We Should Know Better

George Walden has been an MP since 1983. A former diplomat specialising in Russia and China, he has been Minister for Higher Education, a columnist for *The Times*, *The Daily Telegraph* and the *Evening Standard*, and Chairman of the 1995 Booker Prize. His wife, Sarah, is Britain's foremost restorer of Old Master paintings. They have three children.

We Should Know Better

SOLVING THE EDUCATION CRISIS

George Walden

FOURTH ESTATE · *London*

First published in Great Britain in 1996 by
Fourth Estate Limited
6 Salem Road
London W2 4BU

A catalogue record for this book is available from the British Library

ISBN 1–85702–520–2

Typeset by Rowland Phototypesetting Limited,
Bury St Edmunds, Suffolk
Printed in Great Britain by
Clays Ltd, St Ives plc

To my mother,
for her sacrifices and encouragement
in my own education.

Contents

Preface

Some years ago a senior Cabinet Minister asked me with genuine puzzlement why I was so concerned about education. The question surprised me so much I was unable to give an answer. What took me aback was its ingenuousness. The Minister himself was exceedingly well educated. Most of his friends, I would guess, had been to excellent private schools as well. As for the remaining 93 per cent in the state sector, plans were in hand to improve things for them, were they not? So why the fuss?

Years later the 93 per cent are still locked into a second-class system of education. As more of them wake up to the fact, the fuss seems to be spreading. We are approaching an election where education will be to the fore; both John Major and Tony Blair claim to be passionate about it. Yet while the country agonizes about what should be done, the most affluent, articulate and influential people in society will do what they always do when education is debated: having made their private arrangements, they will stand aloof. If education is more politicised in Britain than in analogous countries, there are reasons for it which many find it convenient to ignore, and our apartheid system is amongst the most central.

If some of the judgments in this book sound harsh to conventional opinion on the Left and the Right, the purpose is not to startle or offend. It is simply that any statement of the facts about Britain's schools is bound to be 'offensive' to both Labour and Conservative sentiment, and to the educational establishment. This is because much of the current discussion is characterised by hypocrisy on a collective scale. Facts, the cliché goes, are brutal things, but they make a better foundation for analysis and solutions than the suave or raucous evasions to which we have become accustomed.

The fact that I feel compelled to say something about my own education tells a story in itself. In more educationally advanced countries than our own it wouldn't be necessary: people would judge you by the validity or otherwise of what you had to say, rather than by your social, educational or career background. Yet we start from where we are, and in Britain as it is today it *does* matter disproportionately where you went to school.

I went to a series of state primary schools ranging from Dagenham to Perivale – our most genteel place of residence. Without retrospective romanticising I can claim that they were all old-fashioned places in the best sense, whose working- or lower-middle-class clientele did not prevent them dispensing sound education, maintaining discipline and encouraging ambition. They must have done me some good, otherwise I would not have found myself in an excellent direct grant school: Latymer Upper School in Hammersmith, West London. Subsequently I read modern languages at Cambridge, and added to my education at one time or another in Moscow, Hong Kong and Harvard Universities, and in the École Nationale d'Administration in Paris.

I mention this foreign experience (I was a diplomat for some of the time) because I suspect it too has affected my outlook on English education. Having lived abroad I see the deficiencies of our system more starkly. For super-patriotic Tories this will help to explain my unsoundness on educational, as on other issues. I prefer to think of my years abroad as a chance to compare and contrast, and to see us as we appear to others, without falling into the trap of believing that there are simple remedies to our problems waiting to be imported. No words in this book should be interpreted as meaning that I am an unconditional admirer of either the French or German systems; I see their drawbacks just as I see our own. Each country has its distinct educational culture; the question is not so much whether ours is better than theirs, or *vice versa*, but whether ours is performing at its best. To this there can only be one answer.

This being Britain, I must also 'confess' that my three children have all been to private schools. As I have made clear in education debates in Parliament, my wife and I sent them there for the same reason as many others: because we disagree profoundly with what we see as a philosophy of low aspirations in state schools. It is my impression that there has been progress in our schools here and there, following government reforms, so it would be easy to say that, faced with the same decision today, we would have acted differently. The truth is that we would have done the same.

In this book I argue that as long as our independent sector remains divorced from the national educational enterprise, our state system is condemned to overall mediocrity, and that opening the private sector to all is an essential condition of raising our sights to our potential. To some the proposition will seem outrageous; others will question the means of achieving it. To such critics my reply is: if you deny the existence of the private/public divide, or its nefarious effects on our schools and society, then there is nothing more to be said, other than that we are living in different countries. If on the other hand you agree that a solution is fundamental to our future, but disagree with my remedy, then what is your own? I would be genuinely glad to know it, all the more if it seems to me to be better than mine. At present I see no one addressing the problem, let alone proposing remedies.

In Czarist Russia and the Soviet Union it was believed that people who questioned the *status quo* were mentally unbalanced, or had a grievance against the system. I hereby certify myself to be sound of mind at the time of writing, and grievance-free; it would be useful to have one, in exculpation for my sins, but I am unsure against whom it could plausibly be directed. My complaints are on behalf of others. I am appalled by the waste of talent I see around me, and convinced that Britain has little future to speak of in the world as it is going to be until its public education is raised to a dramatically higher level.

At one stage in the writing of this book, someone concerned with its production sighed and said, 'Sometimes I think it is all too late.' If I did not believe that something could be done I would never have bothered to put my ideas on paper. Like all cultural changes, what I propose would take time. The first step is for clarity and honesty about the situation we are in, and how it might realistically be changed. In education, it is not permitted to despair.

Amongst the works on which I have drawn I would like to acknowledge Denis Lawton's *Education and Politics in the 1990s*; Daphne Johnson's *Private Schools and State Schools*; Bowen and Hobson's *Theories of Education*; Mary Warnock's *A Common Policy for Education*; S. J. Prais's *Productivity, Education and Training*; M. E. Taylor's *Education and Work in the Federal Republic of Germany*; Arthur Hearnden's *Red Robert, A Life of Robert Birley*; and the Institute for Economic Affairs' *Choice in Education* and *A Framework for Choice*. Except where otherwise stated, statistics come from the Department for Education and Employment and the Independent Schools Information Service.

I am also grateful to John Gray of Jesus College Oxford, to Anthony O'Hear of Bradford University, to Nigel Forman MP, to Edward Pearce, to Heads of ex-direct grant schools now in the private sector, especially Dr Martin Stephen of Manchester Grammar School, and to teachers from both sectors with whom I have discussed my ideas. All have been generous with their help and advice, though naturally not all would share my analysis or recommendations. Above all I am grateful to Sarah, my wife.

Part One

Bridging the Great Divide

Chapter One

A Self-doubting Society

'If I weren't Prime Minister I would emigrate.'

(Margaret Thatcher,
in a private moment of exasperation.)

* * *

Britain is a troubled nation: it is clear where it has come from but has little idea where it is going. In both senses of the phrase, it does not know what to make of itself. As it casts about for an identity and a purpose its self-image oscillates between extremes. In the space of a single decade we went from dizzy triumphalism (victor of the Falklands and co-victor of the Cold War, trail-blazer of privatisation, the offshore powerhouse of Europe, everyman's house worth the price of a castle) to near-despair (recession, social disintegration, a despised Parliament, a contested constitution). In a people famed for their sobriety there is something disturbing about these swings of mood. If Britain were a person she would be a suitable case for treatment.

A country that is unsure where it stands in the present will have a hard time delineating its future. How do we see ourselves in the last years of the twentieth century? Honest people have radically different perceptions. Consider these two starkly varying snapshots of the same country:

> Britain is a newly energised nation enjoying one of the most stable and least corrupt forms of government known to history. Free of post-imperial entanglements it has thrown

off its defeatist torpor, eager to engage with the modern world. Its stance towards the Continent is more than a defence of national sovereignty: it is the symbol of a new confidence. Britain has taken painful decisions earlier than others and will soon secure the benefits. Economically it is a gradually brightening beacon for Europe, boasting high growth and employment rates, and a major centre of investment for foreign companies. Talk of a North/South divide overlooks the rapid recovery from decades of de-industrialisation in its poorer regions.

The best of its schools and universities equal or surpass anything available abroad, which is why they are in growing demand by foreign students. It has more newspapers of quality than any other country and its broadcasting standards are the envy of Continental and American audiences. London is fast becoming the most cosmopolitan and sophisticated capital of Europe, while the British countryside includes some of the most beautiful and sensitively preserved in the world.

In literature, the theatre, architecture, fashion, the plastic arts, or the verve of its popular culture, Britain is creative as rarely before, and there is serious talk of a cultural renaissance. Its less quantifiable advantages include a lack of chauvininsm, tolerance, and an inalienable sense of humour. Its habit of self-disparagement disguises what it is too modest to assert: that it remains, today as in the past, the most civilised of nations.

Or:

'Britain is a nation in irredeemable decline. In every field mediocrity has become the high-point of its ambition. Despite years of reform it remains one of the poorer of the European countries in GNP per head, its relative indigence clear from the briefest visit to the Continent. Internationally its influence has shrunk in line with the pound and, with the Cold War over, is shrinking further. As global economics replace the more lordly pursuit of international politics, holding off competition from better-educated and more motivated countries will be a full-time occupation. Its petty nationalism in Europe is a sure sign of insecurity, as patriotism slips year by year into a ratty and defensive jingoism.

Life in Britain is good for those who have as little as possible to do with what is most typical about it: its state schools, its public transport, its charmless conurbations, the tawdriness and infantilism of most of the media. The top few percent of society are internal émigrés: deprived of their inherited or acquired advantages, many of them would emigrate physically, and for good.

As for the tolerance of its people, it is a form of inertia ('indolence of disposition' in Hazlitt's phrase). As for its humour, it is increasingly of the rancorous, self-hating variety. As for its popular culture, to be a market leader in crapulousness is a dubious distinction. In sport, it can't win on the field and disgraces itself on the terraces. Its achievements in literature and the arts are frequently derivative, nostalgic or middle-brow, and invariably overrated. A nation of undereducated masses and dysfunctional elites is destined to be nudged aside by history.

These contrasting perspectives, though my own invention, are not caricatures: the first is based on the officious speeches of Ministers; the second on some of the more despairing writings of cultural and political commentators. To most people, each will have some echo in reality. Forced to choose between them, many might hesitate. Like the double image on a trick postcard, the country slips in and out of focus before our eyes. How we see it at any one moment depends on our angle of vision.

People look at our soldiers in Bosnia, then at our inner-city youth, wondering which is most representative of the nation, and how they can come from the same nation at all. Even allowing for differing political standpoints, the gap in self-perception is colossal. The fact that it is possible to characterise an entire nation plausibly in fundamentally different ways is a measure of our self-doubt.

Disorientation and introversion in the post-Cold War, pre-millennium years are not confined to Britain. Others are taking stock of themselves, and few are content with what they see. France is an obvious example of a country turning in on itself as it seeks, and fails to find, a 'national destiny'. Yet the British are in a category of their own: having risen further in the world than others, our sense of national diminution is all the more painful.

The sensation of shrinkage and insecurity is not confined to chroniclers of decline in the national press. It suffuses our politics and society, the insecurity surfacing in everything from truculent Little Englanderism to (some would say) our new mania for betting. The more we try to dispel it, the greater the uncertainty appears, emerging most clearly in the brittle and self-conscious attempts by the leaders of all parties to 'talk Britain up', as if they were confronting a nation of sullen, discontented children. What few politicians do is to encourage the country to look itself in the eye and to ask hard questions

Outside Parliament many are rethinking the constitution and the monarchy. The crisis of confidence in our institutions has become a cliché, though the relevance of some of the discussion about it can be disputed, and as a form of self-chastisement it can be overdone. For all their baleful symbolism, it stretches credulity to be told that the vulgarity and self-indulgence of a handful of Royals foreshadow the future of fifty-seven million people, or that the retention or abolition of the anachronistic voting rights of a few hundred peers in the House of Lords could swing our fortunes this way or that. Constitutional reform is and should remain an issue, but lack of it should not become an alibi for decline. For all its faults the real problem is not so much our form of governance (there are worse) as the cultural levels and economic efficacy of those fifty-seven million.

To say that the state of a modern nation will depend more than ever before on the degree of enlightenment of its people is to state a sententious truism, yet it is one we have failed to grasp.

If we are to hold our own in a world transforming itself by the day, avoid vandalising our environment and prevent our culture becoming the slatternly handmaiden of market forces, then we are going to have to become far better educated than we are. A small and overpopulated island with few and diminishing resources will be more exposed than more generously endowed countries: increasingly, our skills and our brains will be our only natural reserves.

Even supposing we had it, an 'adequate' system of public instruction would not be enough. There is no future in aiming at technological 'adequacy', or in being a country 'adequately' versed in its own history. Unless it is as a centre of civilised values and high prosperity, with the prestige and wherewithal to defend its interests and exercise a benign influence in world affairs, it is hard to see what the point of Britain will be in fifteen to twenty years' time.

Till now our failings have been disguised by the backwardness of others. At present we are still coasting on the past, dropping the currency as and when necessary, literally and figuratively, to keep afloat. In economics especially, henceforth things will be different: in the space of a single decade one-and-a-half billion people – a quarter of the world's population, from East Berlin to Shanghai – have emerged from their enforced seclusion. Chinese or Russians, Czechs or Hungarians, in their different ways all have sound and long-standing educational traditions, reflecting great cultures. Whether they will come to represent a threat or a promise depends to a large extent on ourselves. Without a superb system of public education to give the country new confidence and a new dynamic (being British we are forbidden to speak of 'a national destiny') our easy ride in history will soon be over.

Except at their peak, 'superb' is not a word that comes to mind as a description of our schools. After years of complacency and self-deception the scale of our under-achievement is becoming more apparent. So ingrained are our adversarial instincts that no agreement exists on causes or cures; should the shadow of a consensus appear, our politicians hurry to dispel it. The question the British should be asking themselves at this stage of their history is not simply 'Which government will be elected and what will it do?', but 'How is it possible to look with confidence to the future in a country where there is not even agreement on the structure and purpose of our schools?'

Our failures become more striking when measured against our potential. Given their temperament, the British should be natural educators. A healthy empiricism, a flair for conjoining the abstract with the practical, a genius for mixing conservatism with reform, an unfanatical approach to religion and open-mindedness to the world – such qualities are not uniquely but pre-eminently British, reflected in everything from our philosophical to our commercial traditions.

Today, in education, it is hard to recognise ourselves. Our minds are inflamed by dogma, our pragmatic instincts strangely deformed. Listening to our petty doctrinal disputations, would Dr Johnson or David Hume recognise their compatriots, two hundred years on? Somehow an entire country has become denatured. When it comes to the policies guiding their schools – and therefore their futures – the British are no longer themselves.

Countries that have benefited from a long-standing educational settlement of the kind Britain so painfully lacks have problems too. The questions they are asking themselves often overlap with our own, as a cloud of doubt descends over Western countries about the nature of education in the late twentieth century. What is the right balance between vocational and academic? What new skills do we need, now that brain power and services seem likely to be the engines of growth in the Organisation for Economic Cooperation and Development (OECD) countries, rather than traditional manufacturing? How many graduates do we need? What is the definition of culture in mass, commercialised societies? And even when it is decided what should be taught and how much is to be spent, how are we to find teachers of sufficient calibre and selflessness to do an increasingly demanding and thankless job?

All this – and the fears of unemployment that underly much of the discussion – has given education a sharper political profile in Western nations. The argument rages in Britain too – though again we find ourselves in a unique situation. When foreigners discuss education they are debating how to enhance their national systems. Britain is different. Unlike them we have two systems of education: one for the top of society, and another one for the rest. And if the atmosphere turns sulphurous the instant the schooling of our children is raised, the reason is not that we are more passionate about education than others. It is that when the English discuss their schools they are talking, consciously or otherwise, about class. And when an Englishman's mind is fixed on class you can get no sense from him.

In our running civil war on education skirmishes come and go. Sometimes it is hard to distinguish who is on which side. When it comes to defining our needs for the next millennium, who are the 'traditionalists', and who the 'modernisers'? In key respects the 'Great Debate' supposedly set in motion by Mr Callaghan's speech at Ruskin College in 1976 never got underway, still less reached a conclusion; like so much else in Britain there seems no reason why anything should ever come to a crunch, and every reason to avoid crunches. Education is one of those arguments which never entirely stops and yet rarely seems to advance. We have got our interminable altercations down to something of an art: a Pinteresque dialogue in which nobody need listen to what the other person is saying because the assertions are as predictable as the responses.

When this or that international survey shows how far we are lagging in maths or physics, or the latest round of national tests brings us face to face with more evidence of calamitous failings in our schools, everyone slips into a well-rehearsed posture. The two sides of Parliament shout at one another; the unions call for cash; the teachers sulk; the press trumpets its outrage; another segment of the middle classes grits its teeth and stumps up for private education; and the public, no longer sure what a good education constitutes any more, having made its genuflections to 'higher standards', shrugs and goes about its business.

In few countries is public discussion so unenlightening and so crudely partisan. In Britain the debate on education is not an educated debate. Our Chief Inspector of Schools, Christopher Woodhead, recently recounted an exchange that took place during the Dearing Review of the National Curriculum ('Education, the Elusive Engagement and the Continuing Frustration', 26 January 1995). Discussing what our schools were to teach, one Head argued in all seriousness that it was pointless to spend time on arcane knowledge that had no relevance to the needs of industry and commerce; another responded with fervour that he wanted his children to know something about our national history and literature. To Woodhead, the primitivism of the dialogue was the most remarkable thing about it. 'What struck me', he commented, 'was that nobody laughed.'

The purpose of our debate on education has not been to refine the arguments but to lay the blame on others, the search less for future solutions than for alibis of failure in the past. Social and political doctrines have dominated the discussion. For parents to teach a child to read before the age stipulated by experts is 'right-wing'. *Not* to teach children the grammar of their own language is good practice on the Left. To acquaint a child with historical dates in sequence is reactionary. To avoid the implication that Christianity has had much of value to give the world, progressive. Sitting in rows is the class configuration of the devil; sitting round tables, the prelude to a new humanity.

Meanwhile a set of brave new doctrines has come from the Right. Market forces and parental choice, we are briskly told, are the elixirs of high standards, education being a commodity like any other. Nationalised schooling can no more work than nationalised railways. The best thing we can do for bright children stranded in the state sector is to toss them a voucher to get to the other side of the line. And, come to think of it, why do we bother with state schools at all?

On radio or television panels one phrase calls forth another with clockwork predictability: A says 'low standards', B says 'resources'; B says 'class sizes', A says 'teaching methods'; A says 'specialisation', B says 'narrow'; A opines that 'some teachers should be fired', B insists that 'the majority are doing a magnificent job'; A says 'selection', B insists that 'we don't want to go back to secondary moderns'. After going a few rounds in the British educational debate the reaction of any sane person is to wonder why he bothered to climb into the ring.

In public or private the exchanges are yawningly familiar. Whether they fall over the dinner table or the despatch box, the words are dead on delivery. It is a pseudo-debate that has little to do with education, and is frequently characterised by class-consciousness, bad faith, self-interest, and above all evasion.

We tell each other – evasively and in bad faith – that class is a thing of the past. In truth all that has happened is that class-consciousness has replaced class animosity, and in education old arguments and resentments simmer on, as incompatible philosophies of society – diversity versus uniformity, 'elitism' versus egalitarianism – react against each other like chemical agents. 'Classlessness' is our soothing alkaline – but the remedy does not work. For 'classlessness' in education turns out to be no more than egalitarianism in disguise. So long as we see our schools as social rather than educational institutions we shall go on fighting the battles of the past.

Now at last there are stirrings of a more candid debate. Slowly we are opening our eyes to reality, and blinking in the truth. A country that only a few years ago accepted without question, with a sort of compensatory national pride, the proposition that 'Whatever you say about the comprehensives, our primary schools are the best in the world' is having to face the fact that, there too, it has been living a lie, and that the charms of informality in the classroom have been bought at the price of systematised low attainment. Even Labour is talking of change, and edging crabwise to the conclusion that our comprehensives have been based more on social doctrines than on the practicalities of education.

All this is progress, albeit from a low base. Yet the old taboos are still there, and the more central the problem the more we shrink from confronting it. Nowhere is our anxious evasion more evident than on the question of independent schools.

CHAPTER TWO

One Country, Two Systems

'We tolerate state schools in the same way that we tolerate brothels.'

(Italian professor to G. V. F. Hegel in 1803)

* * *

To begin a book about education with the question of private schools may seem eccentric. Most studies, speeches or articles relegate the independent sector to the margins of discussion. The reasons appear self-evident. There seems little new to say on the matter. Since the state has virtually no control over them, and since they comprise a mere 7 per cent of the system, what is the point of raking the embers of yet another ancient dispute, except to indulge a grouse? Even that would be a waste of effort. Whether you favour private schools or see them as social evil incarnate makes no difference. Like Ben Nevis or the Alps they are there, in all their impregnability, and will not easily be wished away.

Also, a certain nervousness surrounds the subject. The mere mention of institutions which inflame so many sensitivities, from defensiveness to resentment, guilt to envy, is considered poor form: a mark of bad breeding in itself. As our two-nation system of education becomes ever more deeply rooted, less and less is said about it. Unable or unwilling to contemplate what is happening under their noses, the British behave as they always do when faced with apparently intractable problems inherited from history.

The reaction goes through three stages. First, we deny that the problem exists, or say that, insofar as it does, it has always existed. So why the excitement? Second, we deny that anything can be done about it that will not make matters worse. And third, we claim that, in time, and by processes unspecified, a problem whose existence we are still inclined to doubt will solve itself.

In Parliament a code of silence covers such matters: in debates on education the private sector is rarely discussed. Politicians of all shades of opinion have good reasons to steer clear of the question. If you take the view that independent schools are a sore on the body of British education, unless you have a solution, what is the point of scratching it? Like criticising the monarchy or questioning the basis of mortgage tax relief, whole swathes of the middle classes will conclude that you are talking revolution.

The continuation of our divided – one might almost say segregated – system suits the Left and the Right in different ways. The Conservatives keep 'their' schools intact, while 'old' Labour derives a malign satisfaction from its culture of resentment. The political parties are as comfortable with the public/private schism as they are with the adversarial tradition in Parliament – itself an atavistic reflection of a two-nation culture.

A system where everyone knows their role and their lines has the advantage of dispensing with the need for thinking: you are unlikely to reconsider your position, on schools or anything else, if you can be sure in advance what the other fellow is going to say. Insofar as private education is touched on at all in the course of parliamentary debates, it is one of those discussions that has been reduced to a binary code, the key words in this instance being 'privilege/envy'. You simply press the red button or the blue, and out come the words. There is not much more to it than that.

The idea that things might be otherwise organised in the interests of the country as a whole evokes unease on all sides. For most Conservatives, to raise the subject of independent schools at all can only be ill-intentioned. Private education is like hanging. You are either for or against. There can be no third position. For them the disincentive even to touch on the issue is total. To begin with, in their eyes it isn't an issue. It is a free country and the private sector is simply the place they choose to send their children to school, either because they have been there themselves, or precisely because they haven't. Moreover society, we are reminded, is not standing still: already we have advanced to the point where four out of twenty-one members of the Cabinet have attended one of the schools over which they exercise collective authority (assuming their grammar schools are still there). If, having succeeded in life, they tend to revert to form, like Margaret Thatcher and John Major, and happen to prefer the private sector for their own children, then that is their choice. To describe this choice as a 'privilege' is mischievous, since 'anyone can do the same'. The days have long gone when you depended on social cachet for access to private education. Today it is largely a matter of who is prepared to make the necessary financial sacrifice, and who is not.

So the defensive and disingenuous argument runs. A root and branch hostility to independent education is assumed the moment a question mark is placed against its operation, or unintended effects. Absolute and unquestioning acceptance of the private school system in all its manifestations is a *sine qua non* of allegedly modern Conservatism. Given the wide divergence of views in the party on economic strategy, Europe, homosexuality, hunting or hanging, this in itself is revealing: there is no other subject, not even the monarchy or the future of the House of Lords, where orthodoxy has rigidified into sclerosis, and where new thinking itself becomes unthinkable.

In this instance at least Labour is respectful of Tory prejudice. Such are the tribal traditions of Parliament that many Labour members privately prefer 'red-blooded' Tories, unashamed of their privileges and determined to defend them, to any other variety. It is a world they both recognise, a self-validating world in which each side is defined by its hostility to the other. It is a matter of mutual comfort, a question of manners. Raising the issue of private education in Parliament would be like flouting the rules of a club. One might just as well propose debating politicians' sexual habits.

To refuse even to think about a problem makes it unlikely that it will ever be solved. Yet the state/private divide goes to the heart of our educational condition. Declining to reflect on its consequences is a form of defeatism about standards overall. What we are implicitly saying is that what is incurable is best left alone. The resignation is almost audible: 'With luck we can improve the state sector a bit, though obviously not enough to change things fundamentally, so anyone with the sense and the money should start saving up for fees.'

To discuss state and independent schools in isolation from each other is pointless. Just as the private schools cannot be wished away, assuming that were desirable, so their influence – direct or tangential, active or passive – on the structure and content of our schooling cannot be ignored. To remain blind to the effects of a segregated system is to overlook the defining characteristic of English education, and what distinguishes us most from other countries. The screening out of the sons and daughters of the affluent and influential from the rest of society for their formative years – prep school to university – and the consequent indifference of their parents to what goes on in state schools is more than a traditional quirk in the English system. It severs our educational culture at the neck.

In no other European country do the moneyed and professional classes – lawyers, surgeons, businessmen, accountants, diplomats, newspaper and TV editors, judges, directors, archbishops, air chief marshals, senior academics, Tory Ministers, artists, authors, top civil servants – in addition to the statistically insignificant but eye-catching cohort of aristocracy and royalty – reject the system of education used by the overwhelming majority pretty well out of hand, as an inferior product. In no modern democracy except Britain is tribalism in education so entrenched that the two main political parties send their children to different schools. Only in backward countries is state education viewed and treated as intrinsically second-class, to be avoided literally at any cost. In few developed nations is the gap in achievement between the top and the bottom of society so gapingly wide, and average levels of education so inadequate. Maybe there is a connection?

In our highly sensitive politics of education, even to state what should be self-evident truths will be viewed as provocative. On the Right, you can almost hear the brows beetling. Such things, it will be thought, can only be said by socialists, or worse. The Left acknowledge the facts more freely, though they are not inclined to pursue them. The logic of the academic supremacy of the independent sector leads in dangerous directions. The first result of any serious discussion of the role of private schools is to highlight the inadequacy of the rest, notably the comprehensives, to which the Left is bound by an umbilical cord. The message to them from the middle and upper middle classes is uncompromising: that given the choice we will do anything to avoid sending our children to the average state secondary school, so you had better leave *our* schools alone. 'New' Labour, it appears, has received the message loud and clear.

How did we reach the state we are in? In a sphere which touches on every aspect of life, personal factors are not just relevant but central. Unlike more technocratic fields of government, education is less a matter of politics than of human motivation. Hence the passions stirred by the Harman affair. The degree of self-interest – or social selfishness if you prefer – is greater than elsewhere. Conservative politicians deplore the egalitarian excesses in state education – child-centred teaching, mixed-ability classes, low aspirations and the rest – yet had their own children been subjected to such experiments it is scarcely conceivable that they would ever have taken root in our schools. The wheels of self-interest would have spun with unprecedented velocity and effectiveness.

The wives of Cabinet Ministers would have made their feelings about the 'anti-elitist indoctrination' of their children known to their husbands over breakfast, lunch and dinner. Every Conservative MP in the House of Commons would have been leant on from a great height and badgered by every friend and acquaintance till something was done. Newspaper editorials would have talked of little else. Vice-chancellors would have taken a sudden and highly critical interest in the work of their educational departments, and teacher training especially. In a word, the upper middle classes would have exerted every muscle in defence of what they would no doubt have called a primary right to sound schooling for all.

As it is an experiment which even Labour now admits has been damaging to many of those it was supposed to help, has been allowed to run its course for thirty years. Despite our addiction to sporting metaphors – 'pulling together' and the rest of it – when it comes to education Britain does not play as a team. 'Devil take the hindmost' would be a more accurate motto, and the devil usually does.

Evidence of how elites (used here and elsewhere as a term of convenience) can and do influence educational policies comes from across the Channel. In Germany and France private schools are almost all denominational, and by no means seen as the most desirable place to send your children on educational grounds. The best schools are in the state system, and are used in France by the *grande bourgeoisie* along with everyone else. In Germany similar conditions may have had something to do with the fact that the comprehensive model failed to establish itself widely: it accounts for less than 10 per cent of the system, compared to 92 per cent of state schools in this country, and even then there is more streaming and setting.

When a rash of experimental teaching methods spread through schools in France in the late seventies and early eighties, politicians of the Right and Left joined forces to limit the contagion. One of the most forthright in his opposition to innovative methods was the left-wing Socialist Jean-Pierre Chevènement. Minister of Education from 1984, he became a hero of both the lower and middle classes for his championing of high expectations for children of all backgrounds, calling for a policy of *élitisme républicain* (roughly translated as 'elitism for all'.) The fact that the children of most French politicians attend state schools seems likely to have influenced their desire to maintain their quality. There is great vigilance about standards, accompanied by permanent talk of crisis: the authoritative *Le Point* magazine recently devoted its front cover to the headline: 'Education: the National Failure'. This in a country whose results, academic and technical, are widely seen as superior to our own.

The history of education in Britain over recent decades is strikingly different. Preoccupations with class and sectional interest have been apparent at every stage. It is scarcely imaginable that the Conservative Party would have allowed the majority of grammar schools to be closed and the direct grant schools to revert to the private sector as easily as it did if the children of its leadership and backbenchers had attended them in any numbers. Had that been so it would have exerted itself powerfully in the search for solutions: ways of making the discredited eleven-plus more equitable, improving the prestige of the secondary moderns, and above all finding the resources for a system of high-quality technical education.

What happened was very different. The Conservatives allowed the comprehensives a virtual monopoly of the system with minimal resistance – Mrs Thatcher included, during her spell as Education Secretary from 1970 to 1974. When they protested it seemed largely for the form. However loud their objections against 'levelling down', when it came to the point their self-interest was not sufficiently engaged to struggle against the tide. Personal and therefore political motivation was simply not there.

If anyone was to be 'levelled', it would not be their own children, or those of their friends, but other people's. And when the children of other people are levelled it becomes easier for your own to excel; a no doubt unintended but nonetheless gratifying consequence of segregation. Hence another feature of the British system which, despite progress, still endures: the over-promotion of mediocrity and the under-exploitation of talent.

Human motivation conditions the behaviour of educators too. 'Teacher morale' is another of those problems which, though international, is likely to prove less responsive to treatment in Britain than elsewhere. The causes of low self-esteem include everything from pay and conditions to the shifting definition of the teacher's task and the weight modern societies load on to the shoulders of the profession. In the case of British teachers in state schools it is hard to see ultimate solutions, even when the waves of unrest stirred up by current reforms have subsided.

They will certainly not come from more money or better facilities alone.

What distinguishes British teachers from their co-professionals in Europe is not just the relatively low status of education, though that is a factor. From their first day in the classroom, however gifted or dedicated they may be, at the back of their minds our teachers know that a million of the richest, most influential and frequently most educationally discerning parents in the country will go to any lengths not to send their children to the schools where they teach. They will spend their savings, re-mortgage their homes, borrow money at exorbitant rates, beg cash from aged relatives, drive battered cars and insist that they have always preferred to spend their holidays in Cornwall and the Yorkshire Dales rather than Provence or Umbria – anything to avoid consigning their progeny to the schools used by the majority of their countrymen.

The teachers know too that the top of the ability range – the pupils they enjoy teaching most – will be thinned accordingly, as the 'senior ranks' of society decline to entrust their children to their care. And finally they know that while this situation continues they will never get sufficient resources from any government to do a first-rate job. They may not talk about it much but in their minds they know these things to be true. They are scarcely morale-building thoughts.

The contrast with the NHS is instructive. Whatever its faults it is an internationally reputed service. It too suffers from low morale and complains of a lack of resources (does anyone not?) but those who work there know that the most prestigious hospitals and research facilities are in the state sphere, their excellence open to all, and that the best consultants also work in the public service. You can be operated on free of charge one day by a surgeon who will be treating a Saudi princeling the next. It is scarcely surprising that the English are prouder of the NHS than they are of their schools.

It is of course possible to do a first-rate job in a second-class system, and some teachers do, though the odds are stacked against them. As a profession it is hard to see how they can ever 'deliver', or earn the respect that should be their due. They get much of the blame when things go wrong in society, and none of the praise should something chance to go right. The country as a whole – the moneyed classes included – expects everything of them, yet the top of society will have nothing to do with them. Most will never set foot in the institutions to which teachers devote their lives.

The results of poor morale are everywhere apparent. All professions have their deforming effects – the trumpeting politician, the narky pressman, the oversweet churchman – yet the professional deformations of teachers in state schools are more consistently encountered and more marked than elsewhere. The plaintive, underdog ethos, so palpable from the most casual conversation, says it all. They crave praise but when it comes it tends to be tinged with condescension: 'The vast majority of teachers do an excellent job . . . It is time we began to talk up their achievements.' Politicians and editorialists deem it their duty to treat the teachers like weepy children. As good teachers are the first to recognise, if the vast majority of their profession were indeed excellent, there would not be a problem. Nor would any purpose be served by 'talking up their achievements' when what we want is for those achievements to be more general and more visible. And why should any state teacher feel comforted by praise from politicians or editors who would never dream of calling on their professional services?

How can teachers fail to be aggrieved? However hard they work and whatever their successes they will never feel that they are part of a national educational enterprise, which indeed they are not. Excellence will always be more consistently found elsewhere. They know that however much time they scrimp to prepare a promising pupil for entry to a top university, he or she may well be displaced by a rival of no greater assiduity or intelligence but with a better social and educational pedigree, and the confidence that can come with it. That is one reason why many a teacher is reluctant to aim high. We speak of them as burdened with complexes, but forget that segregation in education on grounds of cash and class is a complex-breeding system: it breeds a sense of inferiority on one side of the line and of superiority on the other. State school teachers are like a football team who are informed at the outset of the season that however many goals they score they are destined to remain in the second league. Again, hardly a morale-building message.

State education is viewed as a field of martyrdom and endless drudgery. The schools where most teachers work have no prestige. There is little glamour in them (where are the educational equivalents of the TV series in which the medical profession is depicted as composed of unsung heroes and heroines?) School buildings are frequently ugly, ill-maintained or antiquated, sometimes all three. Certainly 'there are good comprehensives', but viewed as a whole our schools are seen as a running problem to which there seems no solution. They form a residual system – what is left when you subtract the best institutions in the country. Step inside one of the least favoured and you are surrounded by an atmosphere reminiscent of a branch of social security. Redolent of the ailing society they have helped to breed, their 'remedial' ethos is overwhelming.

Teachers' pay – another standing grievance – is directly related to their position in society. Currently at £22,000, their average salary has kept 13 per cent ahead of non-manual pay since 1979. This sounds more or less satisfactory until it is realised that, judged against other professions rather than against non-manuals as a whole (would doctors be content to be judged against 'non-manuals'?) they have fallen behind. This at a time when expectations of teachers as agents of social stability, as well as instillers of skills and knowledge, have increased.

Even if they were given all they demand – a life free from incessant change, smaller classes, a big rise in pay and better facilities – it is doubtful whether their status or morale would undergo any lasting improvement. Such changes alone would certainly not suffice to bring a million private school parents into the state sector. For teachers would still be faced with the biggest problem of all, which like all the least tractable problems is non-material: how to convince the public of the professionalism of their profession.

Even the most able of our teachers, working in well-resourced schools, have frequently been ill-prepared for a demanding job. Unlike other professionals their training and the theories on which it is based are open to fundamental questioning. Many are burdened from their earliest days in the classroom with an unworkable philosophy of instruction, whose origins are more social than educational, whose methods can smack of alchemy, and whose results are unimpressive by international standards.

The idea that every child can advance at his or her pace by informal, non-competitive techniques that favour spontaneity over effort is a beautiful dream which, lodged in impressionable minds and given scientific status, becomes unconscious dogma. In reality it leads to over-stressed teachers, low aspirations for the gifted and ungifted alike, bored or disaffected pupils, and an enormous waste of time and money.

The contrast with the private sector needs little emphasis. It is not so much a matter of pay and conditions. Although they are not part of the pay machinery of the state sector, independent schools tend to shadow its arrangements; by and large they may pay a little more, but not markedly so. The main differences are where you would most expect them: class sizes, pupil attitudes to learning, a relative absence of difficult children, congenial surroundings. It may be stretching a point to talk about them as two professions – not least since many private school teachers have worked in the state sector – but the difference of attitudes is large. Academically the gap is painfully apparent, and reflected in the larger number of private school teachers who are graduates in their subjects and have a good degree.

The point is not to idealise private schools or their staff. Arrogance, hothouse pressures and social introversion are just some of the negative characteristics frequently to be found in them. To an extent such characteristics are endemic in a closed culture, the inevitable counterpart of equal and opposite failings in the state sector. There, instead of arrogance, there is resentment; instead of hothouse methods, there can be indolence and defeatism; instead of introversion there is passive receptivity to every fashionable influence society has to offer. So our two educational nations mirror each other's faults.

In teaching styles they are driven by distinct philosophies. Private sector methods are, generally speaking, closer to Continental patterns of instruction, described by S. J Prais of the National Institute of Economic and Social Research as 'interactive whole class teaching'. Teacher and pupils are engaged in a joint enterprise, the aim being to bring on the entire group, rather than to ensure that the overall standard is not too demanding, to enable 'each child to come along at its own pace' and to avoid 'divisiveness'. Paradoxically the results in private schools can be more 'egalitarian' than in the state primary or comprehensive system, in the positive sense of raising expectations for all.

To say that the entire apparatus of state education, despite hard-won successes, is second-rate is not an insult to the system, or to the teaching profession: it is a factual observation designed to draw attention to their problems. No good will be done by pretending, for whatever motives, that things are other than they are. Many teachers feel that they work in a second-tier system, and they are right. That is how they perceive themselves, and that is how they are perceived. An OECD study of attitudes to teachers in its member countries revealed that public respect for the profession in Britain was amongst the lowest. (*Education at a Glance*, OECD, April 1995).

Good teachers must share the blame. Self-respecting professionals in other fields – say doctors or nurses – would never allow themselves to be represented in the public mind by people of the calibre of those who dominate some of the teacher unions. The National Union of Teachers (NUT), contrary to appearances, is not a political fringe organisation but has 200,000 members, roughly half the entire profession. Trade unions as a whole are more image-conscious than in the past, and the head of the TUC, Mr John Monks, is a moderate and sophisticated man. Yet teachers hark back to more primitive times. To date the NUT has successfully resisted attempts by its leadership to modernise the face it presents to the public. In an age when we are running out of real-life proletarians there is no shortage of teachers ready to step forward to mime the role. The effect on public confidence in the profession is not good.

Sometimes it is difficult to escape the impression that large numbers of teachers have reached that low psychological point where they no longer care what other people think of them. Teachers' conferences can be like marketing conclaves in reverse. Contemplating the proceedings on television, private school users must cross themselves and think: but for the grace of God, augmented by our savings, our children might have been taught by such people as these. They know there are better people in the system, but are not prepared to take the risk.

Again, it is worth glancing abroad. Teachers with left-wing views have never been wanting in Germany, Italy or France. There, however, socialist convictions by no means necessarily equate with low expectations or whimsical methods of instruction, as can often be the case here. In France and Italy many teachers used to be communists – some still are – but Continental communists tend to be highly traditional when it comes to standards. Determined to achieve the educational and hence social promotion of their pupils, the best of them work on the principle of our own Workers' Educational Association in the nineteenth century: 'Nothing is too good for the working class'.

In Britain the problem of left-wing influence in education is not the political preferences of individual teachers, which are those teachers' business. What is disturbing is the calibre and cultural level of the individuals concerned. On that measure our militant teachers would not be allowed a platform by their fellow leftists on the Continent. They are just not educated enough.

The harm they do to their profession is out of all proportion to their numbers. It is not simply that they are political infants and educational cranks whose speeches and appearance are not designed to bolster public confidence in state schools. The damage goes deeper. By deflecting the debate on education to the unrepresentative periphery they draw attention away from more central issues: what should concern us about our schools is not so much the activities of a few extremists, as the quality or otherwise of the average. Few children are taught by extremists. Many more are taught by inadequate teachers trained in a faulty philosophy of education.

Although the number of teachers who are graduates has increased from 37 per cent in 1979 to 55 per cent in 1996, this must be seen against the doubling of students in higher education over the same period, and the academic qualifications of teachers remain amongst the lowest for any profession. Their lack of prestige is shared by the theorists who guide their work. Educational institutes do not stand high in the regard of their academic fellows, let alone the public; the recent attempts by dons in Cambridge University to prevent a faculty of education being established there reflects more than snobbery and traditionalism. Individual educationalists can be respected, but such institutes and departments are widely regarded in academia as being the resort of undistinguished intellects exercising a dubious discipline, whose capacity for self-criticism is as limited as their prose-style is notoriously obscure.

Though the judgment may seem harsh – good teachers do after all still emerge from training colleges, and there are serious theorists – the impression of institutionalised mediocrity is overwhelming. There is no real dispute about the matter; it is just something that few are prepared to say. The second-rateness is not confined to schools but runs through the entire educational machine from top to bottom.

At the Department for Education and Employment there has long been a problem with the calibre of staff. Attempts to raise the quality of the Ministry's upper levels in the eighties met with limited success: the administration of a second-tier system of schooling is not seen as the summit of achievement on the career plan of high-flying civil servants. Able people have worked there, but on average the quality has not been commensurate with the importance of the work, and on the crucial question of educational philosophies, many are seen as prisoners of the system.

As for Parliament, its debates on education, unlike those on Europe or taxation, are not full to overflowing. Nor is the level of discussion uplifting. Few politicians put ministerial posts in education high on the list of their ambitions. Again, there are exceptions, and distinguished people, such as the late Sir Keith Joseph, have found themselves doing the job. Education committees in the House of Commons do not attract the most aspiring talents. It is not as if their efforts were likely to be crowned with success. For Conservatives, jollying the teachers along is viewed as something of a charitable activity; for reasons too obvious to mention, the element of direct personal interest is unlikely to be there. Pretenders to a ministerial appointment in the Treasury, the Foreign Office or the Ministry of Defence, on the other hand, are not wanting. In terms of national priorities it should, needless to say, be the other way round.

Perhaps the best way to measure the prestige or lack of it of any institution is to listen out for the adjectives used to describe the best of its representatives. State education is one of those fields where the most outstanding practitioners are invariably described as 'dedicated'. It should, and is meant to be, a compliment, yet somehow it carries the wrong associations. Like ambulance personnel, firefighters or lifeboatmen the implication is that teachers are selfless people engaged in a heroic struggle with the impossible. When they succeed in saving a soul we regard them with awe and admiration, and wonder how it is that good people come forward to do jobs like this at all.

Such is the professional standing of those engaged in the transmission of our culture to 93 per cent of our children, and in laying the foundations for the skills and brain-based economy of the future. For a supposedly national system of education it is not a healthy ethos.

In the preface to this book the word 'apartheid' is used to describe our two cultures. To some the term may seem misplaced, or emotive. Yet the comparison is appropriate. Apartheid in its heyday involved a system of 'separate development', the not-so-tacit understanding being that, since one race was inherently superior to the other, the separation would continue indefinitely. Take away colour and coercion, and that is what we have in our schools.

As British people we are discreet about it. It is in no one's interest to acknowledge openly what everyone can see around them, and we have a genius for adjusting our language to circumvent the disagreeable. In polite conversation we try to keep the uglier truths about education from our lips. The hypocrisy that results has become part of what it pleases analysts of behaviour to call our social discourse.

'Not all state schools are bad and not all private schools are good' is a phrase much in use. It is a comforting maxim, frequently pressed into service to distract attention from the central problem. And of course it is true. Everyone knows of cases where parents have spent large sums only to discover that the results bore no relation to the fees paid, the school where they have wasted their money being keener on social than on academic grooming. Equally we can all come up with exceptions to the rule whereby those who can escape from the state sector do so with all possible speed, and where well-off people have contented themselves with local schools, and are lucky enough to have discovered a high-performing institution.

Yet such anecdotes are untypical; that is why they become anecdotes. In our culture of evasion we cling to the exceptions for dear life, and treat them not as proving the rule, but as casting doubt on it. The statement that the grass is green could be equally well contested on the grounds that we have all seen yellow or brown patches. In education, few are in any doubt that the grass is consistently greener on one side of the divide than on the other. What is significant are not the exceptions – the remaining 153 grammar schools out of a total of 3,500 secondaries, the fortunate comprehensives in 'good' areas, the few hundred up-and-coming grant maintained schools (also largely confined to 'good' areas) or the high-performing denominational schools – but the devastating applicability of the rule.

The touchiest question of all is, of course, who goes where. Here equivocation has become a social science unto itself. There exist honest folk who say that they are sending their children to independent in preference to state schools because they think they will receive a better education. Experience suggests that this is one area where honest folk are in the minority. More often it is deemed necessary to invent excuses.

One favourite is dynastical: the child's father or mother went to that type of school and so obviously, therefore, must the child. Another is that private education just happens to be 'more suitable' for the youngster in question – this spoken in a confiding way, the implication being that he or she is of an unusually delicate disposition, and needs sheltering from the bruising realities of the world. Alternatively there are those of a liberal disposition who, having sent their children to a private school without hesitation, rail against everything the independent sector stands for, by way of compensation.

But perhaps the most familiar of our extended gallery of pretexts and excuses is that, while the parents are strong (nay, passionate) believers in state education, their greatest desires have been thwarted through no fault of their own. Given that the teachers are underpaid, the classes too big and the facilities inadequate, they have no alternative but to reconcile themselves to reality and to go for the private option.

At the local level there may well be an element of truth in these complaints. There may also be a touch of snobbery. Either way what is scarcely ever mentioned is the key factor: that the local comprehensive is deemed inadequate for middle- or upper-middle-class needs, not just materially, but because it is not sufficiently aspiring for the children, who will stand a much better chance of attending a much better university and progressing to a much more promising career if their secondary education is bought for cash.

So it goes in our culture of evasion. Hypocrisy is a corrosive thing. Rational people reach the stage when they no longer see the gulf between what they are saying and what they are doing, or feel the remotest need to align their actions with their consciences. Hearing us talk about our schools, foreigners could be forgiven for thinking that cant is indeed an exclusively English vice. It is enough to listen to the educated voices of distinguished participants on radio discussion panels intoning about the advantages of non-selective education. The unctuousness and insincerity evoke echoes of members of the erstwhile Soviet *nomenclatura* prating about peace, or the historical primacy of the proletariat.

The liberal middle classes patronise comprehensives in words but not with their presence. Like the priests of some mouldering religion, they make pious noises in public places, then go their private ways. It is not that Pecksniffery of this order is peculiarly English – one might just as well say that *Tartufferie* is peculiarly French. The point is that, in education, hypocrisy has become the norm.

Such is our native inventiveness on the subject that if a future Labour Government were to shower comprehensives with cash, some other reason for not sending our children to them would be swiftly found. (The fee-paying classes can rest assured: there is little sign that if Labour get into office they would be so rash.) It would be better for all concerned, especially for those who have no choice where to send their children, if parents complained loudly and bitterly about low expectations in state schools before fleeing them. If it is a question of conscience-salving, that would be the most helpful thing they could do for the multitude left behind. But that is not the British way. Educational double-speak has become a part of our lives. And while state schools continue to under-perform, as on average they do, and private schools continue to provide a pay-as-you-enter bolt-hole for our internal émigrés, our little hypocrisies will flourish.

It is not only parents and politicians who find it convenient to turn a blind eye to reality. When it comes to private schools people in the educational world itself are prone to say things that can most kindly be described as intellectual untruths. They are to be found on both sides of the great divide, amongst publicists for private schools, and the professional apologists for state education.

In a recent plea for state support for the independent sector (the *Independent*, 23 May 1996), the Chairwoman of the Independent Schools Joint Council Public Affairs Committee, Averil Burgess, contrasted the funding of private schools in France, Germany and other Continental countries unfavourably with the position in Britain. Pointing out that the proportion of private pupils in France and Germany is higher than here (13 per cent and 17 per cent respectively, compared with our 7 per cent), and that the subsidies they receive are more generous than the £100 million spent on the Assisted Places Scheme, described as 'measly', she lays claim to more money from the state.

The interesting thing about this argument (aside from the deliciousness of 'measly') is not just its effrontery, but its removal from reality. No serious commentator has ever thought to compare independent schools in Britain with those on the Continent. This is because their historical origins and current status are so different as to make comparison meaningless. French and German independent schools, as has been noted, are largely denominational, often academically undistinguished, and by no means the quasi-monopoly of a social and moneyed caste, as is still largely the case here. Their fees are not comparable, their classes are bigger, and in most there is no ethos of exclusivity. Since they are not elite schools in the British sense the absence from the state sector of the parents who use them has little if any impact on standards overall. The plea for state aid for British independent schools is therefore disingenuous. (Objections to the Assisted Places Scheme are discussed in Chapter 3.)

The bad faith of professional opponents of private schools is even more pronounced, as educationalists avert their eyes from the causes and effects of segregation. Baroness Warnock, a former headmistress, solved the problem by writing a book entitled *A Common Policy for Education*, in which the existence of two distinct cultures is scarcely mentioned, let alone discussed. Where, one wonders, lies the element of communality in a policy of separate development according to income and social class?

When educationalists do hint at the truth about private education it is as if they are breaking the news about the existence of sexual perversions to a child. The tone is one of regretful tolerance:

> Some parents may, for a variety of reasons, such as tradition, snobbery or tastes of various kinds, wish to pay for their children to attend a private school. It is a pity that this tradition is so strong in the United Kingdom, even if for

only a small percentage of the population, but, given that tradition, it would not be desirable to close all such schools and forbid that choice.

This was written by Professor Denis Lawton, former Director of the Institute of Education at London University, the most prestigious of its kind, in his book *Education and Politics in the 1990s*. From the pen of a newspaper columnist it could be dismissed as obfuscatory nonsense and forgotten. Given the source, it is an important statement, worthy of analysis.

'Some parents' and 'a small percentage' suggest a coterie of wayward and misguided people. The reality is that the number of children at private schools has expanded by roughly a quarter since the late seventies and now stands at 610,000. 'A small percentage' of parents therefore turns out to mean over a million. And they are not just any million. They include virtually the entire professional and managerial classes, almost the whole of the current (markedly unaristocratic) Cabinet, many a 'champagne socialist', a sprinkling of Labour MPs, and not a few teachers.

The implication that public schools are a special taste and therefore educationally insignificant is strangely unobjective in the mouth of an educationalist; it would strike Tony Blair, who went to one and who clearly benefited from the privilege, as an absurdity. To suggest that the professional classes of an entire country are unintelligent enough to be motivated by nothing more than snobbery and traditionalism in their choice of schooling tells us more about the state of educational studies, and their reluctance to face simple truths, than about the social realities of Britain.

It is a fact verifiable from everything from examination results and university and employment prospects, to the anguished discussions of parents (many of them non-Conservatives) considering sending their child to an independent school that the primary incentive to pay ever increasing fees is to buy a superior education and to avoid an inferior one. For every Ms Harriet Harman who sends her child to a selective school to avoid recourse to the local comprehensive there are thousands of liberal or left-leaning professionals who, after more conscience-searching than she displayed, choke back their tears and their principles and despatch their child to private establishments.

There is no mystery about why they do it, and Professor Lawton's emphasis on social myths rather than academic facts is typical of the genre. A few years ago, a comparison of the examination results between the state and private sectors revealed that, of the top 200 schools in the country, no fewer than 177 were in the private sector. A parent hesitating between state and private schools is likely to be swayed by some of the following statistics:

(1) Eighty per cent of fifteen-year-olds at independent schools gain five or more passes at grades A–C at GCSE level against a national average of 43 per cent;
(2) Eighty per cent of independent school pupils gain three or more passes at A-level against 58 per cent of candidates as a whole. (The latter figure is greatly swollen by the inclusion of private school results.)
(3) Almost 90 per cent of independent school pupils go on to higher education, forming 25 per cent of entrants to all universities. The percentage at Oxbridge is almost double, at close to 50 per cent.

A MORI survey has concluded that amongst the main reasons parents prefer private schools are higher standards, better discipline, and smaller classes. Traces of snobbery and traditionalism are unlikely to show up in such samples, for obvious reasons, though they may not have been wholly absent from the interviewees' minds, any more than they are from the schools in question. Yet 'traditionalism' is not without its positive connotations when contrasted with experimentalism, and allied to persistently good results. The relevant passage in the Independent Schools Information Service (ISIS) handbook is likely to prove attractive to more than a residual clique of social reactionaries:

> Heads and staff at independent schools teach children to work hard and to take a pride in their work; to pay attention to detail; to have good manners; to consider other people's

> feelings and to grow up into responsible adults who will contribute to the community. They wish to inspire in each generation of pupils an appreciation of the richness of their European cultural heritage in music, literature and the visual arts: to lift their eyes above the contemporary to more nourishing cultural experiences.

It would not be difficult to deconstruct this passage in order to demonstrate that 'traditional' in this context means 'elitist'; 'good manners' = upper-class attitudes; 'European' is in implied opposition to 'multicultural'; and 'lift their eyes above the contemporary' means an emphasis on the past in the study of the humanities rather than on the present. To many people who would not see themselves as remotely elitist, in the worst sense of the word, these are valid and defensible attitudes. If the alternative in state schools appears to be the tolerance of slovenly behaviour, undue emphasis on the ephemeral, the inculcation of mass tastes and a moralistic, scattershot approach to other cultures before pupils are familiar with their own, their choice will appear to them to be vindicated, and the sacrifice worth every penny.

If for example formal study of a poem by Donne rather than doodling with the lyrics of Dylan (yes, they can be good) becomes a statement of social and political preference, then there will always be parents ready to pay hard-earned cash to exercise that preference. Other things being equal the result will be that their children will be better educated, if only to the extent that they can appreciate both Donne and Dylan, and understand from critical study why it is that one, all things considered, is superior to the other.

It is interesting to contrast the ISIS statement of objectives with the prospectus of a state comprehensive, selected at random (it was literally the first that came to hand). Norwood School is a secondary school for girls near Croydon:

> Norwood School aims to provide the learning conditions and educational experience through which all girls can

> achieve the highest possible standards in everything they do.
>
> Norwood School is a community in which all members work to guide our girls through the most important stages of their intellectual, physical and emotional growth. In our community all member [sic] are equally valued and committed teachers and support staff work hard to maintain a caring ethos where achievement is celebrated and the needs of girls of varying abilities catered for.
>
> The school values close relationships with parents and the support that parents offer the school in many different ways. It also values close, active associations [sic] with the wider community through many links made with its neighbours, social groups, local industry and prospective employers. We aim to create an orderly community where there is concern for the environment and a positive attitude towards developing the appropriate skills for adult life. Within this context such necessities as self-discipline and a sense of responsibility are frequently highlighted . . . The school is not judged by examination results alone.

At first glance it is hard to quarrel with many of the sentiments expressed in this document. Yet our deconstructor of subliminal messages would have little difficulty in laying bare the underlying meaning.

The first difference between the state and private school prospectuses is one of style: one is written in educationalese, the other in English. One is brisk and to the point, the other sentimental and evasive. 'Learning conditions', 'educational experience', 'caring ethos', 'community' (three times), 'celebrated', 'committed teachers' – the saccharine clichés of the educationalist are all there.

'Heads and staff in independent schools teach children to work hard . . .' says ISIS. An unexceptionable statement, one might have thought, yet at Norwood there seems to be confusion about the purpose of a school. Teachers and pupils are implicitly put on the same level, whereas a school is commonly thought of as a place where the former are superior to the latter: in age, experience, knowledge and judgment. That is why they are put in charge of young people. The pupils go to school to learn and the teachers to teach: it cannot be otherwise.

At every point the emphasis in the Norwood prospectus is on social virtues (the environment, the wider community, 'caring') rather than academic effort. Here there is a certain defensiveness: 'The school is not judged by examination results alone.'

A straightforward comparison between these two documents is of course in some respects pointless. It would be myopic in the extreme not to see that Norwood School, Croydon, is likely to have a different clientele from that of the average private school. It will have inferior facilities, larger classes, and be faced with some of the usual problems that confront teachers in urban schools of mixed ethnicity. Nevertheless the contrast between these two statements of aspiration is revealing, and distressing. It supports the view that our segregated system is underpinned by different values and philosophies. Even allowing for widely varying circumstances and different intakes, it is hard to resist the impression that the essential difference between the two is that, academically, one aims high and the other low.

If private schools were social institutions, mere havens of snobs and traditionalists, there would be little purpose in lamenting a divided system. Private schoolchildren would underperform, their benighted parents would have nothing to offer the state sector, and their non-involvement in maintained schools would be all to the good. Objects of derision, to which no self-respecting parents would send their child, the independent schools would simply wither away.

As it is they have grown steadily. Surveys show that, given the means, many more parents would choose private institutions. The fact that more than half the children who attend them are those of parents who were not educated in private schools themselves tells its own tale. As the social catchment area from which pupils are recruited has widened (partly no doubt as a result of the abolition of grammar schools) their academic superiority over the state sector has increased, and the 'snob' factor has diminished.

Progress is especially noticeable in those young ladies' colleges which were previously more akin to finishing schools than to academic establishments. In 1985 the percentage of girls gaining three passes at A-level in independent schools was far lower than boys: 41 per cent, as against 54 per cent. By 1990 the girls were rapidly closing the gap: the respective figures had grown to 69 per cent and 72 per cent. The trend seems likely to continue, and in 1995 more girls than boys joined day schools in the private sector. (Girls have improved their performance in the state sector as well, though less dramatically.)

The popularity of English private education with foreigners is another argument against Professor Lawton. Fees from foreign pupils currently amount to £200 million per annum and are growing, making the provision of high-quality education a small but flourishing export industry: a niche market in every sense. No doubt the parents include their quota of snobs, upper-class Anglophiles, or whatever you wish to call them. But the Chinese and other Asians, amongst whom places at British private schools are in strong demand (Hong Kong and the Far East are the main recruitment grounds, increasing by 23 per cent in 1994–5 alone) are not educational innocents. They may be rich but they are paying with a purpose.

Insofar as they too are traditionalists they are following traditions of self-improvement through disciplined study prevalent in China for two millennia – a tradition much admired in the Enlightenment period and on which the British drew in establishing the examination-based entry into the Civil Service in the nineteenth century. Soon we shall see the impact of this ethic of application in the economic competition between East and West.

Critics of public schools should be lamenting the fact that a standard of education beyond the means of the average Englishman should be sold to well-to-do foreigners, while the large majority of their countrymen have little option but to resign themselves to an inferior product. No one contests the legitimacy of the trade in high-quality education or the indirect benefits to thc country of this most invisible of exports, in terms of 'making friends abroad'. Yet viewed against domestic reality there is something a little distressing about it. It is as if our best whiskies were kept under the counter, to be produced on demand for rich foreigners, while the great majority of domestic consumers were obliged to content themselves with a less stimulating drink, widely suspected of adulteration.

The view of private education on the Left has failed to evolve with the years. In such eyes independent schools, together with the monarchy and the House of Lords, form the summit of an incurably hierarchical and fundamentally unjust society, doomed to superannuation and decline. If not the source of all the nation's ills they are at the very least undemocratic institutions which perpetuate privilege and arbitrariness in all their forms.

In the case of the Lords and the monarchy, few will deny that they fall easily into the category of what are called 'dysfunctional elites': that is to say institutions which, even if you are prepared to mount an argument in their defence, are patently not working as they ought. Ministers in the Lords, appointed in many instances by virtue of their blood, and by a Conservative Government which proclaims the supremacy of the ballot box noisily throughout the world, are not by and large perceived as the inheritors of superior wisdom, and the esteem of the Upper House suffers a blow whenever the Government whips in backwoods peers to stave off defeat. As for the monarchy, in a democratic age members of the royal family cannot hope to be held in respect if they are no better than the rest of us, and in many respects worse.

But independent schools cannot be lumped together with the Lords and the monarchy. The two circles no longer intersect to the extent that they did. No matter how hard you try (and some try very hard indeed), it is still difficult to buy your way into royal circles, assuming that is where you wish to be. A combination of money and brains will, however, guarantee a child a first-rate education. To that extent private schools are being democratised, even if they are becoming a democracy of the rich and talented. Far from 'dysfunctioning', most private schools have adapted themselves to modernity and are working better than ever before.

The best have understood that social exclusivity is no recipe for academic excellence. Their pupils are by no means always 'superior' people (unless the son or daughter of an accountant is a superior person) though they do receive, by and large, a superior education, and are rewarded with superior chances in life. There are of course poor or indifferent independent schools with little academic ambition, especially in the boarding sector, but there is little point in dwelling on the increasingly atypical.

This is not to deny that private schools can act as transmission belts for snobbery, cliquishness, outmoded social assumptions, or Little Englander conceits. Whether one finds such attitudes more or less distressing than their opposites – the inverted social affectations of many a comprehensive – depends on whether one prefers the flea to the louse, or vice versa. It is possible to recoil from both. As Cyril Connolly wrote in *The Condemned Playground*: 'I hate colonels but I don't like the people who make fun of them.'

The truth about British private schools is not therefore that they are outmoded or discredited institutions poisoning the bloodstream of the nation. If they are viewed as educational rather than as social establishments the problem is the very opposite: it is that they represent by and large 'functioning elites' who are isolated from the nation and therefore in no position to influence its education policies for the better. The difficulty about them is no longer so much their exclusivity – based today less on birth than on money – as their undeniable quality.

To continue to pretend otherwise, whether out of ideological obtuseness or reluctance to re-examine some of the doctrines and values in the state sector, is a form of backwardness in itself, which does no service to English education. Worse, such attitudes embroil us in that most sterile and tiresome of occupations, the English class game.

A society that lacks the will even to confront the facts about its schools will never perceive the nature of the harm done to every side of its life by a segregated system. Consequently it will remain as blind to the need for reform as to how it might be achieved.

Academically, a few figures are enough to suggest the nature and extent of the problem.

	State Sector	**Private Sector**
Number of schools in the UK:	31,000	2,540
Number of pupils:	8,883,000	610,000 (7%)
Cost per secondary pupil:	£2,250	£3,600–8,700 (day)
Pupil–teacher ratios:	18:4	9:8
A-level results:		
% of all A grades, 1994:	59	41
GCSE physics:		
% of all candidates, 1995:	41	59
GCSE physics,		
% of all A grades, 1995:	32	68
A-level, classics (with language):		
% of all candidates:	10	90
Entry to higher education:	27	88
Oxbridge: % of all entrants, 1994:	54	46

These figures could be refined or qualified to infinity: in education everyone works with rough tools, and notoriously subjective judgments. Yet the above statistics are sufficient for the purpose, and have the advantage of coinciding with observable facts.

The caricature of public schools as inculcating defunct cultures can no longer be sustained. Levels of attainment in maths and physics alone demolish our fond image of fee-paying pupils being schooled in subjects suitable for a lotus-eating, mandarin class. As market-sensitive institutions, independent schools have realised – a little late in the day, it is true – that their pupils have to find real jobs in a hard world, where Britain no longer has an empire.

In the nineteenth century, few public schoolboys soiled their hands with the natural sciences; now 35 per cent of ex-private school pupils study science, engineering or technology in higher education, as against 26 per cent for the arts. One of the reasons for the steep rises in fees (which reached an average of 10 per cent annually in the eighties) is the increasing investment of private schools in science and technological equipment.

Nor is it in any way quaint or reprehensible that the classics should continue to be studied. In any event the proportion of sixth form private pupils studying Greek and/or Latin, though providing 90 per cent of the national total at A-level, is a mere 3 per cent. If reading Virgil or Catullus in the original has to be justified in utilitarian terms, one could cite the fact that, armed with keen analytical minds, a high proportion of classics graduates earn large amounts of money for themselves and their country in the City. A good performance in the field does not reveal that an obsolete caste is being schooled in obsolete subjects: rather it underlines the virtual absence of Latin and Greek from the curriculum of even the most advantaged state school; 'classical studies', involving no language, are a poor substitute. Entry to the ancient world, it seems, is by subscription only.

As for the enormous disparity of achievement measured by examination, state school teachers may protest that there is no difficulty in explaining it: they too could attain similar results, if the majority of their pupils were socially and academically select. That is a dubious proposition. To resort to a mechanistic metaphor, it is not just the raw material that matters in education, it is how it is processed. In the case of pupils with low academic potential the 'added value' achieved in private schools can be equally impressive.

A major reason private pupils do better overall is that their teachers have remained largely immune to the social dogmas and experimental methods inflicted on generations of state school pupils (though such are our contortions and inversions that there are independent schools which affect comprehensive values, especially in the teaching of the humanities). If, seen as a whole, teaching styles have remained to some degree in a time warp, experience has shown that education is one area where it is sometimes better to lag prudently behind the fashion than to plunge unquestioningly ahead. It was thanks to its conservative character, based on a nineteenth-century ethos, that education in the Soviet Union was one of the few areas of national and cultural life to avoid calamity under communism. The regime had no hesitation in selecting talented pupils to attend specialised schools, and the achievements of its space and military scientists were not the result of a severely egalitarian order.

Then there is the perennial discussion about resources. Certainly it helps if there are nine pupils sharing scientific equipment rather than eighteen, and better facilities help to attract better teachers. As for class sizes, it is as perverse of the Government to claim that this is of little or no account as it is of the unions to insist that the number of pupils in a room is all-determining. Finally and most obviously, teaching pupils from secure and affluent homes is a world away from seeking to engage the interest and attention of inner-city children whose backgrounds are likely to be more unstable even if they are not economically deprived, who are more exposed to pernicious influences, and who may well be unversed in the rudiments of their own language, even if it is English.

Yet after every allowance for their inbuilt advantages has been made, and after every accusation that private schools risk perpetuating privilege has been accepted, the academic superiority of the system remains overwhelming. It is a cliché of the genre that private school pupils are distinguished by a confidence and ease of manner by contrast with their state school equivalents. The explanation most frequently put forward is the knowledge that they come from a socially advantaged background, but while this remains true of many, it seems unlikely that the sons or daughters of minor businessmen, speaking Estuary English, think of themselves as the product of refined social stock.

A more obvious reason is surely that self-confidence can also be gained by the knowledge of educational attainment. By and large the pupils of independent schools will have been taught to be more demanding of themselves. They will, for example, have read more, not simply because they have more books in their home, but because they have been required to do so. As a result they will have a wider vocabulary – even if they are careful to ensure that it remains largely passive in outside company by behaving like everyone else, and affecting Estuary English.

The danger, as usual, lies in preferring the social to the educational explanation. Looked at from a more realistic angle, old clichés can be reinterpreted in a way that sheds light on our problems, rather than compounding them. 'Effortless superiority' can come from mental effort. 'Ease of manner' can result from an easy ascendancy over people who may be as bright or brighter than the privately educated person, but who lack the articulacy to express their intelligence – an irony considering the emphasis on uninhibited 'self-expression' in state schools. Another advantage enjoyed by pupils from good private schools is that they are less likely to have been encouraged to believe that any form of distinction, above all intellectual, is bad social form. They may affect such attitudes later, with disastrous consequences for our culture, but that is another story.

The purpose of putting stress on things that may appear self-evident is not to induce feelings of guilt in private school users, any more than it is to evoke envy or resentment in the minds of those who cannot afford private schools, or are ideologically opposed to them. Guilt, envy and resentment are not useful emotions. Rather it is to underline the extent to which education in Britain is conducted in two hermetic worlds. And while they continue to be estranged, one will always remain superior to the other

In his recent book *The State We're In*, the new editor of the *Observer*, Will Hutton, comes closer to the truth about private schools than many a politician or professional educationalist. While distrusting some of the values they represent, he acknowledges that they are 'generally educationally excellent', and goes on: 'If private schools could recognise that they were part of the common realm, sharing in common endeavours, then one of the main objections to them would fall away.'

Part of that 'common endeavour' – were it ever to be realised

– would surely consist in the transmission to the state sector of their more positive academic values: the general excellence Mr Hutton so frankly acknowledges.

But this is futuristic. As things are there is little likelihood of such a common realm developing. In the First World War British and German troops climbed out of their trenches to play football against one another. Yet so isolated are private schools in their own sphere that even the sharing of sporting facilities with local councils, or the fixtures that some schools, predominantly in the North, arrange with their state counterparts, are greeted as enlightened and progressive steps.

There is every incentive for private schools to remain aloof from a system imbued with values that are, in so many cases, the opposite of their own. How can the two ever mix? What sort of speech would an NUT official give to a meeting of the Headmasters' and Headmistresses' Conference (HMC) – and vice versa? The idea summons images of farce, or of a plot for a vintage British class comedy. Here are members of the same profession, whose function it is to transmit our national culture, yet who have no common language in which to address each other.

And what advice on national policy on education would the headmaster of one of our great public schools give if invited before a House of Commons select committee? His reaction might be to wriggle out of the invitation, or, if he went, to make pious, non-committal noises. Why should the best schools in the country engage in the debate on education? The Heads themselves – frequently less aloof than they were – may have serious thoughts on the matter. But to the parents of the majority of their pupils, as to the entire upper stratum of society, the pronouncements of this or that party or Secretary of State for Education are matters of indifference. Whatever happens or does not happen in state schools, one thing is certain: they will have no part of it.

It may be advanced in mitigation that parents who use private schools frequently involve themselves in state education (and of course not a few parents have children in both at one time or another). So they do, in a number of capacities, whether as Ministers, school governors, local councillors, layers of foundation stones, or prize-givers. The nature of the involvement is, however, important; given the structure of our schools and society, in the majority of cases it can hardly be other than paternalistic at best, *de haut en bas* at worst. By definition, the school in which the persons in question are moved to show an interest will not be the sort of place they would choose for their own children. Their attitude to it will be conditioned by this knowledge in a variety of ways, most of them negative. It could plausibly be argued that involvement of the patrician variety in state education, smacking as it does of the nineteenth century, is worse than no involvement at all. Predicated on the tacit acceptance of a segregated system it reinforces a quasi-feudal ethic.

It is the custom to describe such people as 'public-spirited' – itself a phrase with patrician connotations, more frequently applied to charitable endeavours. Their attitude to state schools can often be that of benefactors inspecting the results of their munificence with a kindly, self-regarding eye. This would be more tolerable if their efforts on behalf of the school led to higher standards, though that is by no means necessarily the case. Being of a different educational culture they are the last people to draw attention to the system's failings: criticism might well be interpreted as patronising, and as patrician figures on no account must they appear to patronise.

In practical terms this means the unspoken understanding by all concerned that there exist two levels of attainment – one for 'them' and another for 'us' – and that there is little point in pretending that 'they', on average, can aspire to anything of remotely equal quality. While the children of the public-spirited school governor or Conservative politician are receiving a sound education in maths or English grammar at a private institution, children at the school over whose fortunes they preside may well be taught mathematics according to widely contested theories, or spend a lifetime of ignorance as to what an adverb might be.

The public-spirited are more likely to exercise their powers of patronage by raising more money for a sports field, a building extension, or new lavatories. In this way the illusion that all that is needed to improve the performance of state schools is increased expenditure is reinforced. Such selfless actions on their behalf are of course popular with the schools themselves, being equated with 'caring'. When it comes to teaching methods or pupil expectations, our patricians are likely to show every indulgence. Phrases such as 'a lovely little state primary' or 'a marvellous comprehensive' are frequently to be found on their lips, not least if they happen to be Conservative politicians.

Such people would be indignant at the thought that their good works on behalf of the children of others could be seen as in any sense hypocritical. Theirs are the best of intentions. They represent the Marie-Antoinettes of the system, enthralled by the simple rusticities and charming spontaneity of the educational peasantry, and above all enjoying their easy ascendancy over them.

The heading of this chapter – 'One Country, Two Systems' – was inspired by two very different sources. The phrase I have borrowed was coined by the Chinese communists to paper over the economic and ideological chasm between themselves and their Hong Kong brethren in preparation for their takeover of the colony. As it happened, in 1984 a Conservative education spokewoman, Baroness Young, had used a similar phrase to deny any gulf between the state and private sector. Seeking to reassure an Opposition critic in the Upper Chamber, much as the Chinese have been attempting to reassure their doubting countrymen in Hong Kong, she said that education in Britain was 'One system, with two sectors'.

The truth is that it is two systems and two sectors in the service of two different educational nations. There are none so blind as those who have no personal interest in seeing.

CHAPTER THREE

Bogus Solutions

'[In England] certain evils cannot be cured because no one is prepared to talk about them by name.'

(Richard Wagner,
quoted in Cosima Wagner's Diaries.)

* * *

So deep is the gulf separating state from private schooling, and so sensitive the social and political atmospherics surrounding the issue, that it is hardly surprising that the solutions most frequently advanced are either lacking in realism, the result of dubious doctrines, or tinged with bad faith.

Abolition

The least realistic solution is the outright abolition of independent schools, long a fantasy of the political left. In 1965, when Mr Wilson's Government issued the document requesting local authorities to prepare plans for the comprehensivisation of their schools (the famous circular 10/65), the Public Schools Commission was appointed under Sir John Newsome to look at ways of integrating the private schools into the state system. Despite the protests of dissenting members, who warned against 'levelling down with a vengeance', the Commission recommended that integration should go ahead. If necessary, Sir John steeled himself to add, it should be done by compulsion.

For a Government bent on enforcing a single type of education for all, it was a logical step. How could there be comprehensive schools, in both the educational and social senses, if not everyone was in them? Times change. Today it is impossible to imagine such a report being issued, and important to remember the 'brave new world' *Zeitgeist* of the times. It is more than coincidence that at exactly the same period when the Commission was at its labours, serious consideration was being given to knocking down the Regent's Park Terraces, by Nash, on the grounds that the houses were decrepit and could be replaced by something more modern.

It is a matter of history that Labour Governments then and since have done nothing to put the Commission's bold words into practice; the private schools, like the Nash terraces, stand as proud and aloof as ever. Yet the chimera of abolition has never quite dissipated. In 1981 the Labour Party Conference approved a Labour/TUC Liaison Committee document calling for the banning of independent schools, by 7,000,000 votes to 7,000, and since then the abolitionist flag has been raised sporadically by traditionalists in the unions and on the left of the party.

We can be as certain as we can be of anything that should a Labour Government come to power, it will take no heed. Making independent schools illegal is not serious policy. It is the left-wing equivalent of bringing back hanging or the birch: something it is easy to be drawn to in moments of emotion as a panacea for the nation's ills.

The motives of the abolitionists – as of some hangers and floggers – are not always contemptible. Nor is their recipe wholly ridiculous. There are arguments for believing that doing away with private schools at a stroke would indeed improve our national performance (on page 105 I indulge in a fantasy on the subject myself), though much would depend on the policies subsequently adopted in state schools: the abolitionists might not approve of the way an educationally dispossessed elite might exert itself to improve standards. Similarly it could be claimed that a sound public thrashing administered to petty offenders might have a dramatic effect on the crime rate. In many cases it could act as a deterrent to aspiring criminals, failing which hanging would always be there as the ultimate disincentive.

The reason neither of these things has been or will be done is that, however tempted politicians and society may be by total solutions, no Parliament will ever vote for them. The abolition of private education would be both unethical and impractical: wrong on grounds of curtailing individual freedoms and of destroying many first-rate educational institutions; unworkable because the schools would have recourse to law. So great would be their determination to survive that in the meantime many would no doubt take up temporary residence in the disused castles of Normandy, cut-rate weekly returns available for pupils, courtesy of the Channel Tunnel.

Abolition has now entered the realms of party mythology. Labour no longer raises the private schools as an issue, let alone dabbles in solutions; its most recent statements on education have ignored the question entirely. The party's reticence is the more striking in that it has coincided with the expansion in the number of pupils at independent schools; left-wingers could legitimately argue that the greater the problem, the louder the leadership's silence. Even the proposal to review the charitable status of independent schools, which would push up fees substantially by making the schools eligible for VAT, has, it appears, been quietly abandoned. The reason, it must be assumed, is that the benefits to be gained by gratifying the left and raising extra revenue would be outweighed by middle-class votes foregone.

Apart from the commitment to withdraw the Assisted Places Scheme – a move that would have a less damaging effect on private school finances than the imposition of VAT – the Labour Party has now reached a position where it has no plans or policy on how to overcome our segregated system. The only justifications for this inertia would seem to be that:

(1) the Labour leadership no longer believes that apartheid damages education as a whole – a reversal of its historic view that would be hard to rationalise;
(2) it genuinely believes that the problem will wither away as

standards in the state schools rise under a Labour Government and the middle classes are attracted back to them;

(3) it understands the problem all too clearly but is afraid that any moves towards a solution would embroil the party in a row over selection.

If one is prepared to credit the leadership of Mr Blair with a modicum of objectivity, intelligence and social imagination, then the first two of these three explanations must be ruled out.

The Voucher Scheme

Conservative educational ideologues, like their left-wing abolitionist counterparts, have an all-purpose solution to the problems of our schools: vouchers. The object of 'empowering parents' is well known: to increase schools' responsiveness to their 'consumers', to encourage diversity in types of education, and so to improve quality. Painted in these colours it is an alluring prospectus. Surely nothing could be more desirable than to transfer power and responsibility from bureaucrats and governments, widely seen as having done a less than outstanding job in our schools over the years, and to place it in the hands of individuals? 'Choice', 'competition', 'the disciplines of the market' – the slogans are as familiar as they are seductive.

Like most radical ideas, vouchers turn out to be less novel than they seem. There is no shortage of distinguished historical figures to quote on the subject, and everyone from Thomas Paine to Adam Smith to John Stuart Mill – something of a cross-party alliance – has been wheeled on in support. It is true that in his *Rights of Man* Paine suggested that every child should be allotted four pounds a year to attend school; that in his *Wealth of Nations* Adam Smith stressed the importance of the school being responsive to parents and his distaste for public institutions; and Mill took the position that the state should enforce education but not direct it.

Great men as they were, we have a little more experience

of modern democracies. In contemporary parlance what we are discussing is a free market in education. Yet the essential conditions for the operation of anything like a free market are not there. Education is not a 'product' in the normal sense: like broadcasting or the arts it is loaded with philosophical values, history, emotions, and social and economic implications. The voucher lobby appear heedless of this. They talk as if, just as customers for a car will go for quality and value for money, so parents will compare and contrast schools on offer in their neighbourhoods and make rational choices in the interests of their children.

This ignores the objection that not all parents – in some places perhaps not even the majority of parents – have the information or educational background to make sensible choices. Educational vouchers work on the principle of luncheon vouchers, which can be used for a plate of chips and sausages or for something more healthy and nutritious. If people prefer the chips, who are we to condemn them? There are other problems, unfamiliar to Paine and Smith and Mill. In an age when a free market in spouses is increasing marital turnover at a dizzy rate, the incentive of non-biological parents to do the best for the children of whose welfare they have charge, possibly temporarily, can no longer be assumed. Such 'market distortions' are to be found especially frequently amongst the parents the voucher system is supposed to help most: those at the bottom of the social heap.

It is neither 'elitist' nor 'paternalist', but simply commonsensical to wonder whether for example the five million readers of our popular press can be relied upon to select the best school for their children, or whether an abandoned and perhaps severely undereducated mother is in a position to make the optimum 'life choices' for a child whose best interests she may or may not have at heart. It would not be difficult to come up with historical examples where the enforced attendance of a bright child at a particular school has rescued it from a life of material poverty and mental indigence. All this leaves aside the point that it is not the parents who are strictly speaking the 'customers', but the children. And as Dr Rhodes Boyson MP is fond of pointing out, given the choice many children would not go to school at all.

That the present system is too often 'a monopoly supply to captive customers' is undeniable, though the reality is that neither side of the equation can be significantly changed. Even with vouchers the monopoly element would remain in attenuated form, if only because schools cannot be opened and closed like Chinese restaurants, and because of natural inertia. There will always be a market for chips, and in socially deprived areas the educational choice might even shrink. Parents in their wisdom might decide that they were not interested in sustaining a market for foreign languages, literature or the classics, any more than they might patronise a local cinema dedicated to foreign films, or watch opera on TV.

Even in middle-class areas educational utilitarianism is much in evidence, as employment concerns dominate schooling. Ensuring a balance between vocational and broader considerations is one of the reasons a National Curriculum has been put in place – itself a major distortion of the market in the eyes of the voucher enthusiast. One result of anything approaching a pure market in schooling (were there ever to be such a thing) would undoubtedly be to restrict a demanding education in the humanities even more tightly to the private schools than is the case at present, as they came to be seen as a luxury best appreciated by those higher up the social ladder.

Abstract principles cannot be applied in a vacuum, and educational conditions in the UK are highly specific; indeed there is no country like it. If vouchers have been shown to do little to raise standards for those at the bottom in places where the scheme has been tested (the experiment in the early seventies at Alum Rock, California, is the one most frequently cited) then there is even less chance of them working here. In British conditions it seems all too clear what would happen: putting power and money in the hands of the 'consumer' would give another boost to those with actual or potential access to private education. Indeed it is the open aim of some supporters of vouchers, who oppose state schools altogether, that this should be the case.

Most models for a voucher system assume that all parents

would be given the same amount of cash, to be spent at state or private schools. (In the UK this is already being done experimentally with nursery vouchers.) Whatever the consequences elsewhere there seems little doubt that in Britain the results would be retrogressive. Those with children already in public schools would obtain a tax-free handout to finance expenditure they had already undertaken, while those who were able to top up the voucher sufficiently to give them access to private schools would flock from the state system as fast as their Volvos would carry them. Even if the voucher were taxable, the objection of principle would remain.

It is hard to overcome the suspicion that an element of social selfishness, if not outright reaction, may be involved. Edward Heath put it briskly in an article in the *Daily Mirror* (2 November 1982):

> The real motive behind those who continually press for the voucher scheme is to find a way of paying part of the cost of private education by giving a voucher to the parents who already send their children to fee-paying schools. It would cost the government more and not less. And it would be spent on the minority of half a million children and not upon the majority of eight million . . . Education is too important to leave to market economists and to the market.

The voucher lobby might riposte that the transfer of funds from the public to the private domain would be entirely in order, the whole purpose being to allow parents to choose which type of education they prefer. But this is a meretricious argument: in the real world choice would only be available to those who were able to afford it, as is the case at present. The result would be a massive injection of state resources to a socially and financially exclusive sector of education, coupled with a parallel expansion in the number of private schools, and of the pupils attending them.

Supposing the consequences were a rise from 7 to 20 per cent in the numbers of children in private education, it is perfectly clear, socially speaking, who that 20 per cent would comprise. The gulf between the two systems would become wider and deeper than before. An even bigger tranche of the middle classes would have an even smaller incentive to take an interest in the standard of education available to the rest.

In education paradoxes abound. Unconditional admirers of the free market can come to resemble their opposites: absolutists of bureaucratic control. The first insist that all that matters in our schools is the way they are financed; the second that all that matters is that the Local Education Authorities (LEAs) be given more money. In both cases an all-embracing doctrine takes precedence over the practical results on the ground. Cultural factors are ignored or under-estimated, the panaceas each school of thought expounds being ultimately materialistic. Consciously or not both are subscribing to the myth that if enough cash is provided the quality will be forthcoming. What may be true in the automobile market may be less true of education. If it were as simple as that someone would have thought of it before.

The Assisted Places Scheme

Abolition is a non-starter. Vouchers for primary and secondary education are not official Tory policy, and short of a big shift to the right they are unlikely to become so. What, therefore, is the Tory solution for bridging the great divide? Though reluctant to admit that the gulf exists in the first place, the Government nevertheless have a policy to overcome it. This is the Assisted Places Scheme, put in place the year after the Conservatives returned to power, in 1980.

In some senses the Party could be said to have a defensible record on state versus private education. Since 1979 the Government have carried through reforms, for example Kenneth Baker's Education Act of 1988, which are for the most part beneficial. With the exception of grant-maintained schools (though the exact position is in doubt) and the Assisted Places Scheme, the majority of these reforms are publicly or tacitly approved by the official Labour Party.

Seen as a whole, the Government's policies seem enlightened and productive: on the one hand state education is improved through testing, a National Curriculum, extended choice and the rest; on the other, places at private schools are made available to the sons and daughters of the less well-off. Ideally the effect would be a pincer movement which must logically promote greater competition and therefore greater comparability between state and private education to the benefit of all. In practice these parallel policies, far from being complementary, are contradictory.

On the face of it anything more benign than a system designed to 'improve the opportunities for able children from less well-off backgrounds to benefit from the excellent education offered by public schools', as the literature claims, seems impossible to imagine. Here is a scheme designed to lift some 34,000 children from unpromising educational and social backgrounds and to place them, at nil or reduced expense to parents, in some of the most prestigious private schools in the country. Examination statistics tend to support the Government's claim that the scheme is efficient: pupils rescued from the uncertainties of the state sector do well in a more secure and demanding environment. No doubt with Labour's political difficulties about abolishing the APS in mind, in advance of the election the Government have promised to double the money spent on the scheme from £100 to £200 million.

Viewed from a more sceptical stance things look different. The Government's good intentions on the APS are not in doubt. Yet if they had been intent on devising a scheme to give an impression of opening up the private sector to all comers, while maintaining and in some senses reinforcing segregation, they would have invented something very like the APS. An ostensibly enlightened policy turns out on closer inspection to have perverse educational and social effects.

The scheme is aimed at 'helping children who are academically able and whose parents cannot afford the tuition fees for private schools'. The first question to be asked is 'What does "afford" mean?' The answer is that if parents are earning less than £10,000 they contribute virtually nothing to the fees. At around £30,000 (where the scale currently stops) they contribute roughly £5,000 – which assumes that the child is being sent to a fairly expensive school.

Since the average national wage is £17,500, this means in effect that a one-income family on above-average earnings qualifies for assistance from public funds, which is to say from taxes often paid by people less well off than themselves, to send his or her child to a private school. For example a divorced, middle-ranking teacher earning £25,000 a year could receive help from the state to ensure that his or her child does not have to suffer the educational indignity of attending the state school where he or she teaches. This is not an imaginary case.

Statistics suggesting that most recipients of APS scholarships are from poor backgrounds are misleading. For example the Junior Education Minister Robin Squire has claimed that 80 per cent have incomes of less than the national average. Such figures, on closer inspection, are virtually meaningless, the reason being that they exclude capital. You may therefore possess a sizeable home and have a couple of hundred thousand in the bank and still qualify as someone who 'cannot afford the full tuition fees'.

To a Parliamentary question asked by myself as to whether owners of a house worth £700,000 and investment capital of £140,000 giving an income at 6 per cent were eligible for help, the answer was that the scheme was based on 'relevant income from all sources'. Which amounts to an admission that a near millionaire, fallen on bad times though retaining his mansion and a little capital, could qualify. He would not be obliged to exchange his house for something more modest to provide the means to continue to educate his children privately, any more than (until recently) he would have been debarred from claiming his mortgage payments on the mansion from the state.

The stipulation in the APS regulations that 60 per cent of all places must be for pupils from the maintained sector is revealing. Inverted, it means that up to 40 per cent of those gaining assistance could be pupils already attending private schools. Some of these may have been in receipt of scholarships and bursaries provided by the schools themselves (18 per cent of pupils enjoy such assistance). Frequently, however, APS money will go to those who have previously been able to afford fees – hardly in accordance with the spirit of the scheme, as sold to and perceived by the public.

A question mark must also hang over selection methods for places. These are in the hands of the schools themselves. If a child already at a private school is in need of assistance, for example after his parents divorce or get into financial trouble, the inclination of the school to keep the child as a 'customer' will be strong, pretty well irrespective of his or her academic performance. The reluctance to eject children whose parents' incomes drop suddenly is naturally great. It seems reasonable to assume that some of those already in a school who succeed in obtaining APS money might not have been awarded a place if they had been bidding from outside.

At a pinch there is an argument for the taxpayer buying places at first-class schools for first-class, though impecunious pupils. But there can be no argument at all for the taxpayer paying to keep private school pupils of middling ability in independent, fee-paying education. When that happens – as we can be sure it does – the APS is acting as a state insurance scheme for the better-off, for which no premiums are payable.

'The Assisted Places Scheme', the head of a prestigious private school in receipt of APS funds has told me with commendable honesty, 'has in fact largely been used by the ''genteel poor'' or by ''clean-break'' divorcees, or even, at the worst, by Lloyds names (imagine what journalists could make of that!).' Independently of this assertion, the press subsequently turned its attention to the workings of the APS, unearthing some egregious cases, including families with large country houses and two or three children benefiting from the scheme.

Like other MPs I have seen examples of the wholly legitimate exploitation of the system by middle-class parents. Telling applicants who approach their MP for advice that the scheme is not devised with people like them in mind cuts little ice; suggesting that they move to a smaller house to help pay their private fees cuts no ice whatsoever. The expression of indignation in their eyes at these moments is the clearest reflection imaginable of middle-class rapacity. It is a look that says: 'I have a right to it, so I am going to claim. I will do anything to keep my children out of state education, and I am not going to enquire too closely into who foots the bill.'

Since the awards available are frequently undersubscribed (a result of parental ignorance or teacher resistance at lower social levels), less deserving applicants who can by no stretch of the imagination be described as poor often succeed in their applications. Not long ago I received a Christmas card thanking me warmly for helping a parent with a magnificent house to get an award for the continued education of her child at the taxpayer's expense, when in fact I had done nothing at all. She had simply applied and got the money. It is unashamedly said by Conservative MPs that however arbitrary the scheme in its application, politically it is efficient, since 'our people like it'.

An even more fundamental objection to the APS is its defeatism about state education, which is implicitly written off both for the present and the future. (The scheme has now been extended to primary schools.) The message it conveys is that state schools, be they in deprived or middle-class areas, are incapable of nurturing the talents of able children. The fact that this may indeed be true in specific cases, and that the child performs better in a private school, makes no difference to the argument: the impression that state schools are irredeemably second-rate, a place all who are able flee at the first oportunity and by whatever means available, is increased. Whether its beneficiaries come from inner cities or verdant suburbs, the underlying philosophy of the APS is an admission of failure. The signal it sends out is *sauve qui peut*.

The Government say that while handing out scholarships to private schools they are simultaneously attempting to raise standards and diversify opportunities in the state sector, so encouraging fruitful competition between the two. This claim is invalidated by a third objection.

It is no secret that a number of private schools have faced financial difficulties in recent years. It would be pleasant to believe that this results from the increasing counter-attractions of state schools, though sadly there is little evidence that this is the case. The reasons independent schools can encounter problems include generally rising costs, financial insecurity amongst parents, and the gradual run-down of the armed forces, whose children were educated at boarding school when their soldier-parents were serving abroad. The effect of these pressures has been a slight falling away from the peak the private sector achieved just before the onset of the recession in 1990 (the latest figures suggest that this is being reversed).

In this uncertain situation the APS has become a more valuable indirect subsidy to the sector than before, and its doubling over the coming years (assuming the Conservatives are still in power) has been greatly welcomed by its potential beneficiaries. To speak of 'keeping the private system afloat', as some have, would be a wild exaggeration of the difficulties faced by the sector, which give every appearance of being temporary. Yet the least one can say is that £100 million a year spread amongst the 300 or so schools currently participating in the scheme is a handy amount of money.

Financially, then, the effect of the APS, albeit at the margin, can be to help sustain the division between the state and private sectors. Educationally, the result is the same. If the premise that state schools will never reach their potential while they are ostracized by rich and influential parents is accepted, to build up the achievements of the independent sector by creaming off talent available from the state and paying for its schooling can only reinforce the blockage. Seen in this way the APS becomes a circular, self-perpetuating policy: the state sector will never be good enough for brighter children while these self-same children are despatched to the private sector, whose very existence militates against higher standards in state schools. A policy designed to make breaches in the wall separating public and private in fact shores it up.

The scheme was launched with honourable aims, its perverse

effects probably never considered. It is not difficult to understand the oversight. There are certain mindsets that are hard to break. The APS no doubt sprang from genuinely charitable instincts in the Conservative party, but such instincts are an unhealthy guide to action in modern societies. In Dickensian England its introduction would have been a progressive measure; today the scheme has a grace and favour, 'charity child' whiff to it, all the more suspect if the child in question is undeserving of public charity in the first place. The promising 'scholarship child' is thrown a life-raft by his or her betters, for which he or she is duly grateful, which he or she uses to swim to a higher educational and social station, and everyone is content. Merit is rewarded and the Tory Party can proudly display its one-nation credentials.

In essence it is a patrician policy, and patronage runs deep in the Tory soul. The trouble with patronage is that there is one who gives and one who receives: in vaunting itself as a one-nation policy the APS is implicitly acknowledging that, in education, there are two. The subsidising of private schools by the state helps to ensure that the twain shall never meet. The idea that all children could have a *right* to go to the finest schools in the land, assuming they display the necessary talent and diligence, and that this right forms part of society's educational enterprise, is alien to old-fashioned Tory thinking.

Had the scheme been devised as the first stage in a strategy aimed at the gradual extension of choice to the entire private sector, it would have been a genuinely far-sighted measure. There is no evidence that this was or has become the case. As shown by the recent decision to double the funds to buy places under the APS in advance of the election, the thinking is short-term, and strictly political. Even when it is doubled it will offer 65,000 out of 610,000 places. And how many of those awards, it is permissible to wonder, will go to the best-qualified and most needy pupils?

Labour motives and actions on the APS are the mirror image of those of the Conservatives. Left to themselves there seems little doubt that the right wing of the Party would allow the commitment to abolish the scheme to lapse, or be hedged round with benign conditions (this may yet happen). To withdraw a direct subsidy to something in the order of 50,000 voters (double if one includes those aspiring to benefit from the next £100 million), many of them middle-class, is hardly in line with Labour electoral strategy. It must be assumed that their persistence in this policy is largely dictated by negative reasons: were they to rescind it, as they have the threat to withdraw charity status, they would have no policy to satisfy their left-wing or the teacher unions on private schools at all.

Labour promises to transfer the £100 million saved on current expenditure to state schools, to 'buy excellence for the many rather than the few'. The slogan is on the same level of intellectual honesty as the Conservatives' claim that the APS opens the private sector to the deserving poor. Ex-APS pupils will have to be educated in the state sector, which will cut the savings almost by half. The remaining £50–£60 million pounds, sprayed over nearly 10,000,000 pupils, comes out at roughly 12p per pupil per week – hardly enough to buy much in the way of excellence, always assuming 'excellence' can be bought for cash alone. Nor is there anything wrong in principle with promoting excellence for the few. That is what all governments do by financing fees for our cleverest students at our best and most costly universities.

If Labour had a positive programme to erode the public/private divide their stance on the APS would be more acceptable. There is indeed a case for withdrawing the subsidy, for the reasons argued above, but that case only makes sense in the context of a wider strategy. As it is the Government have succeeded in driving Labour into an old-fashioned 'anti-elitist' stance, at a time when thoughtful people in the Party are trying to evolve a more sophisticated position on education.

Once again the adversarial tradition, by which the policy of each side is devised in reaction to the other, has won the day. The APS, conceived as a 'bridge-building' initiative, has turned out to be as divisive in Parliament as in schools. We are back to push-button politics, the red and the blue, and the crude simplicities of 'privilege/envy'.

Do Nothing: State Schools Will Catch Up

If it could be convincingly demonstrated that state schools are improving out of all recognition, and that current reforms will ensure that they will improve further, till a critical point is reached where a majority of parents return to them from the private sector, then the entire thesis of this book is exploded. Whatever the non-academic attractions of private education, people would not be inclined to continue to pay high fees for a similar or identical 'product'. The examination record of the state sector would soar, the prestige of the independent sector would decline, the numbers would shrink, and private schools would become in reality what they are said to be now by their opponents: a sanctuary for snobs. Unfortunately this seems an improbable scenario.

How is the state sector performing today? The assessment of politicians of all parties is paradoxical. On the one hand they stress how bad things are; on the other they enthuse about progress. The Prime Minister is on record as saying that 'The top 15 per cent of youngsters who come out of our schools are equal to anything you will find anywhere in the world. The other 85 per cent frankly are not.' Assuming the 15 per cent include the 7 per cent of pupils at private schools, the Prime Minister is claiming a modest 8 per cent success rate in the country's maintained schools, judged against international standards. That is not an encouraging report of progress after a decade and a half of reform.

The perception by Labour is scarcely less gloomy. In a reflective speech to the Social Market Foundation (26 February 1996), the Opposition Education Spokesman, David Blunkett said: 'In spite of more than fifty years of universal state secondary education and thirty years of comprehensive education, the pattern of excellence at the top and chronic under-performance at the bottom persists.'

As the election approaches Tony Blair too is making increasingly critical speeches about our schools, warning that 'Equality must not become the enemy of quality'. From a different standpoint, in essence Labour are confirming John Major's views.

When politicians are moved to say similar things – albeit for dissimilar motives – it becomes worth listening.

Scepticism returns when the same politicians insist, a little too clamorously for comfort, that things are improving beyond measure. So it is whenever GCSE and A-level results record an increase in successful candidates, as they have done each year till 1995. The rate of progress claimed has become preoccupying. In 1975 23 per cent of candidates obtained five O-level or CSE equivalent subjects at A–C grade. In the first year of the GCSE the figure was 26 per cent. Currently it stands at 43 per cent, an increase of almost 50 per cent in nine years.

In 1985 11 per cent of the seventeen-year-old population obtained three or more passes at A-levels; ten years later the figure had doubled to 22 per cent. Naturally the progress these figures were said to represent was welcomed by almost everyone who had anything to do with education. Doubts about the maintenance of standards were widespread in the press, though with the exception of John Patten, who as Secretary of State was undiplomatic enough to hint at grade erosion, no official misgivings were expressed about the marking or rigorousness of the examinations.

It is not difficult to understand why. Some teachers and pupils may indeed have deserved their improved results, and would feel understandably resentful at having the quality of their work impugned and the value of their certificates implicitly downgraded. But the real reasons for the failure to enquire too closely into whether or not standards were being maintained were the demands of educational politics. The Conservatives were obliged to demonstrate that their reforms were working; Labour was obliged to interpret better results as a consequence of teacher commitment in the face of a niggardly and misguided government; and the educational community can always be relied upon to protect its own.

Now the doubts have filtered up. In 1995 an enquiry was established into the maintenance of standards over time, under the School Curriculum and Assessment Authority, concentrating on English and maths; it has still to report. Its findings, however, have been to some extent pre-empted by the results of the Dearing Review of Education from 16 to 19, announced in March 1996. The conclusions were manna to the sceptics. Some of the most popular subjects at A-level, such as English, business studies and art, were pronounced insufficiently demanding.

Maths and physics were said to have held up their standards – which may help to explain why there is a shortage of A-level candidates and of university students in each. (The numbers of applicants for each place at Cambridge for example are English 4.1 per place, maths 2.4.) The overall impression is not just that too many pupils are choosing 'soft' over 'hard' subjects, but that the 'soft' ones may be getting softer. Sustaining sunny reports of progress in state education in the light of the evidence of the Government's chief advisers, be they Christopher Woodhead at HMI or Sir Ron Dearing at the Schools Examination Assessment Council (SEAC), becomes difficult. And if Labour seriously believe that schools are improving their performance, why have Tony Blair and David Blunkett begun to question the philosophies on which they are based?

It may be objected that this is a mere examination-based snapshot, and that reforms take time to work. Complaints about state schools are broadly twofold – low expectations and inadequate resources – and it could be plausibly argued that there are actual and potential improvements in each area. Spending per pupil has increased by 45 per cent in real terms since 1979 (a figure to be treated with caution, since fixed costs tend to inflate it); and the Government have introduced elements of competition and choice which, over time, could reinvigorate the system. Many comprehensives are somewhat less doctrinal in their teaching methods than they were, and in particular it is suggested that grant-maintained schools, released from the dead hand of the educational bureaucracy, could one day pose a challenge to the independent sector.

Already there are grant-maintained schools in existence whose determination to break free from the drab norm is impressive. After securing their independence such places can blossom overnight. Anyone who has visited the more successful grant-maintained schools 'before and after' cannot fail to be struck by a new sense of pride and purpose, whose fruits may not be confined to the facilities and physical organisation of the school. Propelled perhaps by an inspired, independent-minded Head, with a nonconforming (i.e. non-egalitarian) teaching force and highly motivated school governors, a new beginning can be effected.

This is especially likely to occur if the schools in question operate a selective entry system of one kind or another. Eighty-one of the 641 opted-out secondary schools were already grammar schools. Some of those who were not have changed their status to become wholly or partly selective (twenty-one have so far done so, with another five applications pending). Others may operate a semi-clandestine policy of selection: grant-maintained schools tend to be oversubscribed, and parental commitment to their child's education can be used as cover for singling out the most promising pupils. Whether selection is overt or covert, partial or whole, academic results can be expected to improve in proportion.

It seems possible that, in time, such schools could attract some of the potential clientele away from the independent sector. Those worried about taking on commitments at a time of job insecurity, or those with a conscience about sending their children to private schools could see them as an attractive alternative. Yet the number of such high-aiming grant-maintained schools is likely to remain small, and inevitably they will be concentrated in middle-class areas. Even at their best they are hardly likely to improve on the performance of the remaining grammar schools, themselves inferior to private schools in overall levels of achievement. If Labour win the election the future of grant-maintained schools is uncertain, especially those with a selective ethos. And whatever happens private schools will continue to offer superior attractions in the form of class sizes and facilities.

In many grant-maintained schools opting out could bring few changes. Some have done so largely to avoid closure on the grounds of falling rolls. Others will become independent more in body than in spirit. Their main incentive to break links with the LEAs in the first place may have been to claim the extra resources (genteelly called a dowry rather than an inducement) dangled before them by the Government, with which to extend their facilities. Such externally prettified establishments may have no high academic ambitions. They will resemble those reconditioned council flats that sprout balconies in gaudy colours but where essentially, life goes on as before.

The best test of an opted-out school is perhaps how much use it makes of the most potent provision in the regulations governing it: the power vested in the governing body to hire and fire staff, and the availability of government money to pay for redundancies ('Guidance to Promoters of Grant Maintained Schools', paragraphs 44–5). The difficulty of ridding themselves of underperforming staff, in the face of resistance by their union and the tergiversations of the LEAs, has been a long-standing grievance amongst more ambitious Heads. By selecting a team of teachers most likely to raise academic sights, an energetic Head, supported by his or her governing body, can swiftly change the ethos of a school.

The number of grant-maintained schools who avail themselves of this freedom will be a rough and ready test of the vitality of the new sector, and therefore of the inroads it will make in a market dominated by private schools. So far the evidence is not encouraging.

Despite inflated examination results and the tendency of the Government to talk up their own achievements, both of which make it hard to come to an objective assessment, it is nevertheless possible that state schools are progressing overall. Yet it is important to keep a sense of perspective. What is the aim: excellence or adequacy? And where do we start from? Apologists for comprehensives say that many have abandoned mixed ability teaching. If that is progress, then ceasing to bang one's head against a brick wall is progress too. It will take far more than that to reassure those who are sceptical of the entire comprehensive doctrine. What worries them, not unnaturally, is how comprehensives could have carried on doing it for so long, and why they ever began.

Meanwhile private schools are not standing still. Even if state schools are improving and continue to do so, the gap with independent schools could grow. In both sectors the reputation of individual schools can go up or down. The recession has forced a number of closures of private establishments (the most recent figures show that fifteen have folded since January 1995), yet these tend to be amongst the smaller institutions, and do not include prestigious names. Overall the sector has demonstrated the resilience and adaptability one might expect from what are in effect private enterprises; in the same period, for example, there were eighteen mergers. The remarkable thing is not the fall-off in numbers since the peak year of 1990, but how well independent schools have weathered the storm.

The strain on less wealthy parents is worth recalling. The average cost of educating two children at private secondary day schools is £9,000 annually, say £13,000 earned income before tax and national insurance payments. Yet despite the collapse in house prices, widespread negative equity, and job insecurity that has affected the South as well as the North, and earners in the middle and upper brackets as well as those lower down, the proportion of those willing to pay fees for their children's education fell by a mere 0.4 per cent (7.5 per cent to 7.1 per cent) in the years after 1990.

The latest figures (ISIS Census, April 1996) show the first overall rise for four years, of 3,000 pupils. New demand for day places has more than compensated for the fall in boarding school numbers, itself more than made up for by increased demand from overseas. Such figures do not suggest that independent schools are under siege from a resurgent state sector.

As for examination results, private schools go from strength to strength. If the success rate claimed in the performance of state school pupils is beginning to cause concern, in private schools it is positively alarming. In 1985 the percentage of pupils leaving with three or more A-levels was 48 per cent. By 1995 it had leapt to 85 per cent – as against 16 per cent in state schools. No doubt the improvement owes something to the increased preoccupation of private schools with academic results, and to the higher aspirations of girls in particular. Nevertheless the leap is spectacular. The figures bear out the concerns of the former High Master of St Paul's School, London, now Lord Pilkington, who some years ago expressed the view that A-levels were becoming too easy for independent school pupils. His solution was that the sector should establish its own, more challenging system of examinations.

The proposal was not endorsed by the Headmasters' and Headmistresses' Conference (HMC), though many of its members believe that the grades awarded at A-level have become inflated. As a result the HMC is considering ways in which able pupils can be more stretched. Their ideas include:

(1) persuading universities to recognise a credit given to a student in his or her first year for additional work done during the A-level course;
(2) keeping the 'S' (scholarship) system running and recognised by universities;
(3) the introduction of additional modules for subjects like maths for more able students.

Allowances must again be made for the natural advantages of the sector. Yet the idea of private schools increasing their demands in response to the dilution of academic standards, while laudable in principle, is a poor augury when seen in a wider context. It hardly supports the view that the public and private spheres are drawing together. Rather it amounts to the institutionalisation of the two educational nations, with a higher peak of attainment for the affluent, and a lower one for the rest.

The conclusion seems clear: like abolition or vouchers or the APS, waiting for the state sector to 'catch up' and for the two sectors to converge is the politics of illusion. Under a Conservative Government which subsidises independent schools, and whose policies, though tending to raise state school standards, will not and cannot match aspirations and resources in fee-paying schools, it seems probable that the independent sector will retain its easy superiority for the foreseeable future, and that any change will be at the margin. There is certainly no sign as yet of a shift amongst the children of Conservative Ministers or backbenchers from one sector to the other.

As for the possibility of a change of culture in state schools in the longer term, while the possibility is not to be written off now that Labour have joined the Conservatives in questioning the non-competitive ethos, the powers of resistance of LEAs, the teaching profession, and educationalists should not be underrated. It is they and not the Government who run our schools, and the absence of the most demanding and articulate parents from the state system will do nothing to hasten progress. Conservatives are curiously blind on this point. They lay heavy emphasis on the benefits of parental involvement in state schools, yet refuse to see that while the top of society boycotts them they will never work as they should.

To that extent the question as to whether they can ever 'catch up' is circular, a chicken-and-egg argument to which there is no end in sight. The task is Sisyphean. As the natural champions of independent education, of continuity and acquired rights, it is questionable as to how far Tory hearts are in it.

A gap that has widened under the Conservatives is unlikely to narrow under Labour, whatever its bold words on the need for reform. Should Labour in power persist in its plans to reduce the autonomy of grant-maintained schools, hold ballots amongst all local parents on whether to close grammar schools and generally give primacy to the comprehensives, it is not just improbable but impossible that the state could ever close the gap with the private sector.

Those in 'old' Labour and the unions who claim that it could, provided the comprehensives were given sufficient resources, are mere romantics. The word is not used lightly. It is not a matter of opinion, but of simple logic. The adherents of a completely comprehensive system are in fundamental contradiction with themselves. Even if a Labour Government invested the massive sums the comprehensives insist that they need, without basic changes in their philosophy of education the middle classes as a whole will never use the schools, and cannot be forced. And if the remaining grammar schools are closed both they and the majority of their pupils' parents will probably go into the private sector.

There is a second contradiction. Supporters of comprehensives also insist that they can never fully succeed till all classes send their children there. But under any likely future conditions the whole of society never will. Therefore comprehensives can never succeed while they aspire to be comprehensives. The promoters of uniformity in our national education are caught in the logic of Groucho Marx.

The element of circularity in the positions of both political parties lends an impression of unreality to the debate. We could go on like this for ever. Unless we break free from the vicious circle, we probably shall.

CHAPTER FOUR

Opening Up

> 'Everyone complains about the weather but no one does anything about it.'
>
> *(Mark Twain)*

* * *

The argument of this chapter is based on four premises:

(1) No country has evolved a high standard of public education while the top 7 per cent of its citizens, however defined – the elite, the successful, the affluent and influential, *la classe gouvernante*, the *nomenclatura* – have nothing to do with it. There seems no reason to suppose that Britain will prove an exception. International comparisons of achievement suggest that it will not.

(2) Involving the elite in the common educational weal would raise expectations overall – though much would depend on how it was done. To do it by compulsion would be unworkable; to do it by 'levelling' would defeat the purpose.

(3) A bridging of the state/private divide would not of itself solve all the problems in our schools. A parallel strategy is essential to raise standards in the state sector. In addition to current reforms, this would involve a major rethinking of its philosophy and teaching styles, coupled with a greater financial priority for education. One without the other – a greater investment in an unreformed system – would yield few results.

(4) The twin strategies in state and private education are complementary. The will for a steep increase in the performance of our schools will not be there until the whole of society is engaged in the enterprise. Conversely, reforms and more public spending in maintained schools will not of themselves eliminate the gap in expectations and achievement between the state and private sectors.

So much for objectives. In practice three rules must govern any attempt to bind our fractured system together. The first and most fundamental is that change should be driven by educational rather than social motives. The worst failures in British schools have occurred when these priorities were reversed. The high standards achieved in private schools must on no account be compromised, though they can be further enhanced.

The second rule is that change must be voluntary. Independent schools have an absolute right to their independence. Apart from any moral objections to compulsory change, legally it seems improbable that any measures that infringe their autonomy would be enforced in the courts. The third rule follows from the first two: since no blueprint for redrawing the line between state and private schools can or should be imposed from above, overnight solutions are neither possible nor desirable. To take root, a new status for independent education would need to be gradual and organic, and based on existing schools.

The notion of attracting private schools *en bloc* across the line into the state sector is unrealistic to the point of fantasy. Inviting them to join a new sector of education, specifically designed with their needs and traditions in mind, would stand a greater chance of success. The principles governing its membership would be:

(1) Any private day school which satisfied the necessary academic criteria could volunteer to become part of a third force in education. This might be called the Open Sector of Independent Schools. Boarding schools, which form only one-sixth of the private sector, could join only if money was made available from private sources to cover the extra costs.

Existing maintained schools (e.g. grammar schools) would not be eligible.

(2) Open Sector schools would open their doors to all, regardless of income or social status, by aptitude and ability.

(3) The financial and academic independence of such schools would be guaranteed by charter. Any co-operation between LEAs and Open Sector schools would be on an equal and voluntary basis.

(4) The finance for such schools would come from a mixture of private and public sources. The money allocated under the APS would henceforth only be available to private schools who volunteered to enter the Open Sector. Public finance would not be channelled through local authorities, but go directly to the schools

The formation of an Open Sector would be an accretive process. Though they would be technically eligible to join (assuming boarding costs were covered) the scheme would not be aimed primarily at the old public schools, such as Winchester or Eton. These are the schools most prominent in the public mind, but they are far from typical of the sector as a whole and form only a small proportion of available places. In the initial stage, ex-direct-grant schools now in the private sector – a very different category of institution, many of them no less academically distinguished – are more likely to be attracted by a change of status.

There are currently 120 former direct grant schools in the independent sector. Together they account for nearly 100,000 of the 250,000 private secondary places, and historically they have found themselves at the fulcrum of our state/private system. Before they were effectively compelled to integrate fully into the private sector in 1976 such schools played a special and highly significant role. Neither entirely private nor entirely open to pupils from the maintained sector, they straddled a frontier which has since become demarcated with greater precision. Seen in the light of our present, sharply polarised system, their more liberal history is instructive.

In pre-Second World War days roughly 10 per cent of state pupils moved from elementary schools to county grammar schools via what was known at the time as 'the Scholarship'. Where insufficient grammar schools were available 'Scholarship' winners were allowed to apply for entry to direct grant schools. These were fee-paying institutions theoretically in the private sector, but received a capitation grant directly from the government to accept pupils whose fees were paid by the LEAs.

The 120 direct grant schools cover every major conurbation in the country, from Newcastle and Merseyside to Sevenoaks and Truro. The relative lack of grammar schools in the North of England earlier in the century helps to explain the strong tradition of ex-direct grant schools in that region. The demand for high-quality secondary education from the skilled workers and technocrats servicing the engineering and other industries at the time was also a factor. The excellence of such schools, drawing as they did for talent on a wide social swathe, is summed up in the names of Manchester Grammar, King Edward VI School for Boys, Birmingham, Latymer Upper School, Haberdashers Aske's, or Alleyn's School, London.

The practice of using the direct grant schools as a sort of overflow system for qualified pupils was formalised in 1926. The 1944 Education Act subsequently stipulated that 25 per cent of places in direct grant schools should be free and filled by pupils educated for at least two years at maintained or grant-aided primary schools, that a further 25 per cent or more places could be reserved by the LEA, and that fees for the remaining places should be on a sliding scale. The Government also helped with capital costs.

This '50/50' approach was in keeping with the schools' status, betwixt and between the two sectors. For half a century – from 1926 till Mr Wilson's Government forced the great majority of them fully into the independent sector in 1976 – they played the role of a half-way house. They were not designed as such at the outset: this was no piece of deliberate engineering from above but a gradual, semi-improvised response to educational demand, which grew organically. In that sense they were an example of enlightened pragmatism. People saw that it benefited everyone to make some of the best education in the country available to the most promising pupils, from whatever background. 'Brain not pocket' was the common-sense criterion of the day.

In the more ideologically charged atmosphere of the sixties and seventies the schools came under growing pressure from the Left, in whose eyes they were an irritant, conforming to no rational blueprint. At a time when class politics dominated educational thinking to an even greater extent than today, the direct grant schools were seen as bastions of privilege which had somehow intruded themselves into the state sector. There was as little room for their selective ethos in the monolithic concept of comprehensives as there was for the grammar schools, the large majority of which were transformed into comprehensives, beginning in 1965.

The consequence of the abolition of almost all grammar and direct grant schools in the space of little more than a decade was a dramatic reduction in the educational opportunities open to bright children from modest backgrounds. There has been endless argument and debate about the social motivation behind these reforms: educationally, for the academic child, a single statistic on university recruitment supports the view that the impact was retrogressive. In the late sixties the highest A-level grades achieved by pupils admitted to Oxford and Cambridge Universities belonged to applicants from the direct grant and maintained (i.e. largely grammar-school) sectors. Today it is the independent sector – 7 per cent of the system.

A scattering of grammar schools has remained, and a handful of the direct grant schools of a Catholic denomination chose to make the necessary adjustments and remain in the state sector. Broadly speaking, however, in two of the most divisive measures in our educational history – the famous circular in 1965 calling on LEAs to discontinue selection, and the abolition of direct grant status in 1976 – the secondary system was effectively polarised between private and comprehensive schools.

*

The direct grant schools suffered a lingering death, as Labour and Conservative Governments came and went. In the Second Report of the Public Schools Commission published in 1970 the direct grant schools had been offered two alternatives: they could either be funded by central government, or be assimilated into local arrangements. In effect it was Hobson's choice: either way they were to cease accepting fee-paying pupils and to become, over time, non-selective. When Reginald Prentice, then Labour Secretary of State for Education (he was subsequently to defect to the Conservatives, for educational amongst other reasons) announced the decision to abolish the schools to the House of Commons on 11 March 1975, his Conservative shadow, then Norman St-John Stevas, described the decision as a piece of educational vandalism, and went on:

> Finally, will the Rt Hon Gentleman note that the Opposition pledge to reopen the direct grant school list still stands and that we reaffirm it today? Will he also note that we shall rebuild the bridge between the independent and the maintained sector which he has so rashly sought to blow up today, and that we shall see that the schools are not only restored but restored on a legal basis which will make it impossible for them to be destroyed again by ministerial edict?

This commitment, no doubt heartfelt at the time, has never been honoured. Instead, when the Conservatives won the 1979 election, the Assisted Places Scheme was brought in: a measure quite different in its strategy, and more welcome to the private sector as a whole. As with grammar schools, in retrospect it is hard to avoid the impression that, for whatever reasons, the Tories in effect colluded with the Left in blowing the bridges.

Conservative policy on schools during the period was characterised by incoherence and indecision, and one must be careful about attributing devious motives where there were probably none. It has to be said, however, that an overwhelming majority of Conservative Ministers and backbenchers, both then and today, have not been personally inconvenienced by the abolition of the direct grant or grammar schools. It is permissible to speculate that, had the threat from the Left been to the independent sector, Conservative politicians might have exerted themselves somewhat more energetically in its defence. If Labour had accepted the advice of Sir John Newsome's Public Schools Commission and found some way of abolishing private schools in the sixties, there is little doubt that the Conservatives would have resurrected them, with as much haste as appeared seemly, the moment they returned to power.

Meanwhile the revolution in secondary education had been decisive. Standardisation advanced in swift and resolute steps. In 1971 35 per cent of all secondary schools were comprehensive, and by 1981 the figure was 90 per cent. Whatever their motives or intentions, the out-turn was as clear as it was satisfactory to each of our major political parties. In the division of spoils both had secured what concerned them most: the Left had its cherished comprehensives in place, and the Right had its private schools intact.

Enticing the former direct grant schools into a new Open Sector would do far more than restore the *status quo ante* 1976. Their status would be clear. There would be none of the quotas for state pupils imposed in the 1944 Education Act. Nor would the schools be obliged to accept pupils according to their ability to pay. They would recruit purely on the basis of merit. They would not simply obscure the boundaries between the two sectors, as they had done before: as free-standing institutions in an Open Sector, offering a first-class education to all, they would act as a beacon for the remaining independent schools. Over time they could open the way to an evolution towards a single, mixed educational culture, with access to schools of all types open to all on a basis of aptitude and ability.

Objections from the Left and Right are not hard to foresee; our traditionalists wear heavy boots and one can hear them coming. Anticipating their arguments may be a useful way to clarify what is proposed.

Why Should Any Private School Worth Its Salt Enter the New Sector?

The notion of private schools opting to join an Open Sector would indeed be pie in the sky if there were no sign of interest amongst the schools concerned. Reactions from the Heads of the 120 former direct grant schools now in the private sector to the idea of a new status suggest that there is. In 1995 I wrote to each one of them to canvass their opinions, and their responses are instructive documents. The Heads in question are an exceptionally experienced group of people, better able than most to provide an overview of the educational state of the nation that transcends tribal camps. A large proportion have been educated in maintained schools themselves (often the grammar sector) and many have taught on both sides of the line.

Virtually all the replies expressed interest, however modified by caution, in the possibility of change. Many were clearly unhappy with the present status of their schools, even though most are performing well in recruitment or examination terms. The dominant feeling was that they were not discharging their educational responsibilities adequately in the private sector, and that the vocation of both the Heads and their staff lay elsewhere. Their responses imparted a strong impression that they and their schools had been forced, against their inclination, on to the wrong side of the line.

As statements of educational conviction the letters were remarkable. The following passages are taken from different letters:

> 'I have never wished to work in the independent sector . . . For twenty years at least I have been expressing the view that so long as the most powerful, the most affluent, the most influential and articulate can educate their children outside the state system, nothing will happen that would seriously change perspectives and improve standards in the state system. If those same people had a personal stake in

the state system it could, and no doubt would, improve overnight . . .'

'It grieves me that the fees we have to charge disqualify so many from benefiting from the education we provide . . .'

'If ever such an offer [i.e. of a change of status] was on the table I would consider it, together with my governors, very seriously indeed.'

'. . . so many pupils motivated to progress in the intellectual world but deprived of an opportunity to pursue it . . .'

'The greatest step forward in the quest to raise standards in our schools would be the opening of the former direct grant schools of Britain to all pupils of academic potential . . .'

'It was only with the greatest reluctance that in 1977, in order to maintain the school's character and independence, the governors decided that the school should become fully independent . . . I and my governors would be very interested in restoring a situation in which the education we offer could be made available to children from the widest possible range of backgrounds . . .'

'The proposals are fascinating. At the moment we have roughly 250 applicants for 25 Assisted Places and it is hearbreaking sorting them out.'

Many Heads set out minimal conditions for change. The coincidence of priorities was striking. Broadly speaking, there were three:

(1) a guarantee of continued ability to select;
(2) a guarantee of autonomy, especially on teaching styles;
(3) the ability to ensure that per capita funding would allow them to continue to offer their present levels of education.

On point (3) it was clear that, if necessary, some would be ready to sacrifice a certain amount of financial independence, on the common-sense premise that any funding from the state would have to be accountable. But there was a marked reluctance to become victims of what they saw as the bureaucracy and inflexibility involved in central administration.

Lest the quotations reproduced above sound too much like a series of blurbs, I should add that some Heads voiced reservations. Only one was of principle. His fear was that for such schools to opt into a new sector would not bridge the public/private divide, but simply displace it: i.e. that the division between state and private would be reproduced by a division between selective and non-selective schools. The point has some validity though the distinction – between an open and closed system – is a big one.

One or two Heads believed that vouchers in some form might be the answer. Another preferred 'closer links' with the state sector to any form of new status. Not a few were wary of political interference (hardly surprising after the experiences of direct grant schools in 1976) and unconvinced that Labour, with its rooted antipathy to selection, would either initiate or tolerate such a solution. A number had a higher than usual proportion of pupils under the APS scheme and were nervous about any threat to it.

The most positive reaction came from Manchester Grammar School. A legend of high achievement (25 per cent of its pupils go to Oxbridge), it is considered the flagship of the former direct grant sector. Its High Master, Dr Martin Stephen, with the backing of the school governors, has publicly expressed a readiness in principle to change status. In a statement given front-page treatment in *The Times* (28 February 1995) Dr Stephen said he would: '. . . support any move to research the possibility of our becoming once again a part of the maintained sector . . . The Manchester Grammar School believes that the education that it offers should be available to all regardless of their parental background, and subject only to its pupils passing the entrance examination.'

After this announcement a number of other formerly direct grant schools – notably King Edward V1 School for Boys, Birmingham – indicated sympathy with Manchester's move.

Developments following the Manchester initiative were a parable of parliamentary inflexibility and immobilism. Although I had forewarned the Prime Minister that Manchester might be prepared to review its status, and had written to Tony Blair and Paddy Ashdown on the subject (texts and replies in the appendix) the announcement by a school of Manchester's eminence appears to have caught the leaders of the political parties by surprise. Media comment saw it overwhelmingly as a bold and imaginative gesture. Parliament moved swiftly to squash it.

In a reply to a question from myself the Prime Minister showed no awareness of St-John Stevas's commitment to restore the direct grant sector in response to the announcement of their demise by Reginald Prentice. Perhaps he was simply without background briefing (which would be surprising since the story was front-page headlines in *The Times*). Whatever the reason, far from welcoming the development, or indicating polite interest, John Major appeared to go out of his way to turn Manchester down.

So the Party that had deplored the enforced flight of the direct grant grammar schools to the private sector as 'educational vandalism' went sharply into reverse at the news that the most famous amongst them might be interested in coming back. In a subsequent adjournment debate the Junior Education Minister, Robin Squire, implied that the reason for the Prime Minister's lack of enthusiasm was largely financial. The most charitable explanation of the Government's negativism is that they understood the significance of Manchester's move all too well, and were afraid that words of welcome for Manchester might only encourage other private schools in the same direction.

Aware no doubt of the incongruity of a socialist party declining an opportunity to open the doors of a private school to all the talents, but bound by the party taboo on selection, Labour's reaction was prudently non-committal. Its Education spokesman, David Blunkett, followed Major's example by hastily pushing the ball into the long grass in the course of media interviews, trying not to sound negative but making orthodox noises about selection. The Liberal-Democrats kept their heads down. So it was that Manchester, which had made its move at the cost of some raised eyebrows amongst the parents of its pupils, had the door shut in its face.

The response on both sides of the House was not unexpected: Manchester had broken loose from the established conventions and was cavorting about in the wide open spaces between the tribes. The fear of change was mutual and instinctual: if pupils were to be chosen by merit to go to one of the best schools in the country, where would it lead? Manchester's move was an unwelcome intrusion into a hermetic debate, whose rules and boundaries were fixed by tacit agreement between the two sides of the confrontational system. It was the political Establishment closing ranks against the public interest.

Left to themselves the responses of the Prime Minister, Blair and Ashdown might have been different – though this is less certain in Major's case. I know from a conversation I had with him at his request about my proposals that Blair, while constrained by party orthodoxy, is more open to new thinking. But perhaps not just yet.

If They Want to Change Their Status Private Schools Are at Liberty to Do So Already

Technically, this is correct. Section 51 of the 1993 Education Bill made specific provision for any independent school to enter the state sector as grant-maintained schools, should it be so minded. There are few conditions. The Bill merely stipulates that 'account would be taken of the character of the proposed school' – the purpose being to have regard to the existing varieties of school in the area in question.

It is easy to see why this provision was included in the Bill. Politically there is every advantage in being seen to welcome private schools to the grant-maintained sector (such as building bridges and breaking down barriers). The reality is different. The fact that only two schools (St Anselm's College, Birkenhead and Upton Hall Convent School, Upton, Wirrel) have so far availed themselves of the opportunity (applications from two Muslim and one Seventh Day Adventist school are pending) speaks for itself. The reasons for the lack of wider interest are plain. Joining the state sector on grant-maintained terms would mean that the school received grant-maintained funding. Few if any private schools could manage to maintain their class size, grounds, excess teacher costs and traditions on approximately £2,500 per pupil per year. Opting into the state sector, albeit with the relative independence that comes with grant-maintained status, would also involve a formerly private institution subjecting itself to the full panoply of the law governing those schools.

It seems unlikely that this section of the Bill was inserted with any visionary expectations of luring the private schools over the line in mind. It is little wonder that it has remained largely a dead letter, its 'progressive' nature ignored, its existence scarcely remarked.

Who Would Finance the Open Sector?

The economics of the new sector would be a key consideration in making the proposal politically saleable. Eroding educational apartheid and opening a new layer of choice to all would be popular amongst voters of all parties – though not all voters have children at school. For them the political attractions would diminish in rough parallel to the expense.

However it is done, the establishment of an Open Sector would not be cheap. Cultural change of the magnitude contemplated cannot be achieved without cost. When the need is clear, society pays the price without hesitation: the 'buying out' of a declining mining industry and an entire way of life associated with it in Britain, France and Germany at the cost of billions of pounds spent on redundancy packages and retraining facililities is an example fresh in the memory. In education the cost would be of a lesser order, though the implications of change would carry greater significance. Moreover the cost would be spread over time as more and more schools entered the system, and there are ways to distribute it so that it would not fall entirely on the Exchequer.

The differential between the state and private sectors of secondary education is currently in the region of £2,250/£4,500 per year (the exact figure is obscured by, for example, capital costs). It could be argued that any child selected for entry to a more expensive sector of education had as much moral right to full state funding as a pupil gaining entry to a university, where the fees – whatever the parents' income – are paid by the general taxpayer. He or she could be claimed to have earned their place by virtue of their ability and effort.

In the real world there are three reasons why it would not be possible for the taxpayer to finance the Open Sector entirely. First, the extent of the bill. At present something in the region of two and a half billion pounds are spent in private school fees, including prep and boarding schools. Should a majority of Secondary day schools eventually transfer to the Open Sector the cost to the Exchequer would be large, especially when taken together with the extra expenditure on state schools proposed in the second part of this book. Such a sum spent on an 'elite' would give rise to the same objection raised by Labour over the APS: 'Why not spend the money on the state sector to improve standards for all?' The fact that the objection would be unsound would not prevent it from being made, or from evoking an echo in the general public.

Second, objections to the state financing the Open Sector outright would be the greater if it were perceived that a high percentage of pupils who gained free places came from those who had previously paid fees. This is the famous (or infamous) 'dead weight' principle close to the heart of the Treasury, one of whose tenets is that the Government should never finance activities people have shown they are already willing to pay for privately. In this case public perceptions might be on the side of the Treasury.

In practice the rule is not watertight. There are at least two recent precedents – both in education – which demonstrate that when the pressures are on to secure a change of attitudes, the 'dead weight costs' taboo can be overridden by determined politicians. The first example was in the establishment of the students' loan system in 1990, under which well-to-do parents who had previously received no help from the state with the maintenance costs of their student children were given access, along with everyone else, to interest-free loans which resulted in extra costs to the Treasury. The thinking was of course that the cost was an acceptable price to pay to implant the idea of student loans in the public's mind. Similarly with the current experiment in nursery school vouchers, where middle-class parents already paying for private nurseries received a most welcome hand-out from the state, to the tune of £1,100 per child per year.

Yet it is possible to over-refine the discussion. In the real political world, however persuasive these two cases may appear as precedents, they are mere debating points. Given the sensitivities surrounding private education it would be neither understood nor appreciated if even a handful of well-to-do parents began to receive free, from one day to the next, a 'privileged' education for which they had previously been ready and willing to pay.

Therefore there must be other sources of finance. The first contribution to the cost of an expensive new sector of education would have to come from the parents themselves. Inevitably this would involve a system of means-testing. The word provokes an instant mental recoil, though it is hard to see why: the concept is central to our entire financial culture. Progressive taxation is 'means-testing' of the most intrusive kind. The principle is well established in higher education, where there is a sliding scale for maintenance grants, the poorer students getting the full amount available and the better-off nothing, apart from their interest-free loans. Complaints from parents who were used to paying would be unlikely: they would be too thankful that their children had been selected for a place. Moreover in the case of former direct grant day schools the fees are relatively modest (£3,500–£5,000 per year), and on a sliding scale some might pay less than they do already.

The objection that there is no tradition of fee-paying outside private schools is both inaccurate and irrelevant. It is inaccurate because parents who were able paid full fees at grammar schools in the early part of the century; it is irrelevant because the point is neither to maintain nor re-invent tradition but to encourage fresh thinking to solve a specific problem. New modes of financing public expenditure are already accepted on both sides of Parliament. Under the codename of Private Financing Initiative, public and private interest comes together in the financing of infrastructure.

Applied to a new sector of education the principle would be broadly similar, and reflect the more flexible and realistic spirit of the times. Pupils in the Open Sector would be receiving a more costly schooling than others and would contribute accordingly where they could. To those who could not the cost would be free.

Despite surface similarities there would be no comparison with the Assisted Places Scheme. In one case scholarships are handed down from above, granting (supposedly) poor children free entry into a closed system; in the other, pupils from all backgrounds would gain places by virtue of their diligence and ability in a system open to all. They would not have to demonstrate that they were poor enough to be awarded a place, and so deserving of public charity, but be admitted *as of right*. It is the inverse principle.

The third source of finance would come from the abolition of the APS. Private schools might complain of undue pressure to goad them into joining the Open Sector, yet it would clearly be anomalous to continue to finance a scheme to which there are strong objections of principle and practice once a more equitable and enlightened policy was in operation. Buying places in private schools while simultaneously trying to attract them into adopting a new status would be contradictory.

The finances for an Open Sector would therefore come from three sources: some of the parents themselves, the APS money, and the remainder from the Exchequer. Private gifts and donations, for example, from local industry, would be uncovenanted bonuses, on which the schools would not be dependent. In the initial years, when a limited number of schools would apply for entry, the cost would probably be covered by a combination of fees and the savings from the abolition of the APS. Thereafter the additional costs would fall to the taxpayer.

On a rule of thumb – much would depend on how many schools entered the scheme and how many paid fees – that cost could eventually be of the order of one billion pounds a year: one-third of 1 per cent of annual government expenditure. There would be little difficulty justifying the extra expenditure politically, and no feeling that money was being poured down a black hole. The benefits would be apparent to all, not least physically. All over the country prestigious schools, previously closed to the majority, would provide more choice for all. As each formerly exclusive establishment threw its doors wide they would inspire a sense of communal pride, becoming 'our' schools instead of 'theirs'. The feeling of a country's education growing together would increase. It is hard to think of a field where the money could be more profitably, or more visibly spent. (Off-setting cuts in government spending are discussed on page 187.)

Would Not the Same People as Before Gain Access to the Open Sector?

To some extent, yes. There is a natural and inescapable correlation between social and educational advantage: more stable households; well-educated, aspiring parents; awareness of opportunities, etc. Such factors can never be entirely eliminated in any society under any system of schooling, even if it were thought desirable to do so. Good-quality nursery and primary education could add to the advantages of birth. These factors would, however, tend to be diluted over time, and evolution speeded up by:

(1) the improved provision for state schools discussed in the second half of this book, including the establishment of nursery education for all, higher pay for teachers, etc;
(2) changing teaching styles and raising standards in state primary education;
(3) increasing awareness amongst parents of the new opportunities for entry into the Open Sector;

(4) a diminishing hostility amongst teachers against grooming a child for access to a 'privileged' education (which acts as a drag on the APS), such access now being open to all.
(5) the Open Sector would judge candidates on their potential as well as their performance in examinations, in the way already practised in interviews for university places – though without recourse to positive discrimination which would become self-defeating by lowering the standards of the new sector.

A New Type of School at the Top Would Do Little to Remedy the Problems of the State Sector as a Whole

In the short term, this is true. To achieve a rise in standards and opportunities in all schools simultaneous reforms would be needed in the state sector. A voluntary democratisation of private education would nevertheless have effects disproportionate to the size of the sector. It is important to think through its practical effects.

The first consequence would be that already high-performing schools, such as the former direct grant schools, would become even better in the Open Sector, relying as they would on recruiting the most able pupils, irrespective of ability to pay or social background. Drawing on the best talent available would push their achievements above those of the average independent school, which by its nature contains a complement of students of mediocre or low ability. Private schools who chose to remain outside the new sector would find themselves, for the first time in their history, in something approaching a true market. The APS subsidy would be gone and they would be facing real competition – with all that meant for A-level scores, university entry, attracting the best foreign students, and their general prestige. How they met such competition would be up to them.

Once a significant number of private schools had opened their doors to all by selective examination, many at the top of society might find it less easy than before to find a niche for their children as new talent displaced them. At present such people compete for places amongst themselves. In the Open Sector they would be competing against all and sundry.

Parents who had hitherto experienced little difficulty in obtaining a place in a formerly private school, and whose child failed to qualify for a place in the Open Sector, would be faced with a choice. Either they could continue to buy education in a fee-paying school which had not entered the new sector, or was not considered of high enough quality to be accepted; or they could search for a suitable school in the state sector.

Staying in the private sector could entail the acceptance of a relative drop in standards as time went by. For parents such as these, buying a privileged path to higher education for their children would become a tougher proposition. Searching for a suitable state school, should that be their preferred solution (much would depend on individual inclination and level of income) would mean closer involvement in the maintained sector. The experience could only be salutary for all concerned.

As the Open Sector flourished the remaining private schools would find the strains of keeping up with it increasingly demanding. The result could be a domino effect throughout the system, as more and more schools reconciled themselves to joining the new sector to maintain their standards. Should the end point be reached where the best of the private schools had decided voluntarily to enter the Open Sector, the displacement effects in the upper reaches of society would become significant. Put simply, privileged people would no longer be able to count on gaining entry to the best schools in the country by wealth, influence, and social position alone, and would find themselves taking a new and constructive interest in how the other half lives.

Why Spend Money on Elitist Schools at All?

Such might well be the response from many on the Left. The simplest rejoinder to the 'anti-elitists' is to turn the question back on them. What is your alternative policy on private schools, given that abolition is a fantasy, and that they seem unlikely to wither away? How else do you propose to erode the apartheid educational culture you so loudly deplore?

Reluctance on the Left to consider an Open Sector would revolve around a rooted objection to selection in any form. Such atavistic reactions inhibit thinking. The slightest mention of selection, for whatever purpose, is deemed to equate with a full-scale return to the grammar school era. It is as if a ban had been pronounced on the sweeping of chimneys on the grounds that they had once been swept by eleven-year-old children long, long ago.

To allow this instinctive antipathy to dominate Labour policy on private education would be tantamount to accepting the indefinite continuation of things as they are; rather than do something to resolve the problem, Labour would be seen as preferring to nurse a grudge. The fact is that no private school of any academic distinction is going to enter the state sector as a comprehensive. This may be right or wrong of them, but either way they are not going to do it, and cannot be forced. Reluctance to abandon selection was the cause of the direct grant schools 'defecting' to the independent sector in the first place; given the record of comprehensive education since then, they are unlikely to revise their opinion.

Labour's vision has always been of a single educational culture. Some favour comprehensive uniformity, others a more variegated system. Either way they have no means to achieve their objective of greatly improved standards for all. Morally they are therefore in the position of the man who demands higher pay for everyone, but has no answer when asked how this most enticing of prospects is to be achieved. The challenge to the Party on our educational structures is ultimately of greater importance than Clause Four. There was never a realistic prospect of the Labour Party in government re-nationalising old state industries – telephones for example – let alone new ones. Schools' policy, on the other hand, is a clear and pressing problem.

Other than to retain and modify Conservative reforms here and there, Labour has no answers. Its position on selection and private education, seen together, is highly paradoxical, not to say contradictory. When all the evasion is stripped away what it comes down to is that Labour is ready to see the continuation of elitism in the worst sense: to tolerate selective admission to the best of our schools by cash and social position, but not by ability. Labour would do well to measure its policies against the words of R. H. Tawney, the Party's most celebrated thinker on equality. In his famous work *Equality*, published in 1931 and later updated, he wrote of:

> . . . the barbarous association of differences of educational opportunity with distinctions of wealth and social position. It is the habit of treating the public educational system as of secondary importance, which that association inevitably produces. It is the refusal, as a consequence, to introduce into it the improvements which all practical educationalists know to be long overdue, as though common children were lucky to be offered any education at all, and could not reasonably expect to enjoy the same range and quality of opportunities as their betters. The hereditary curse upon English education is its organisation upon lines of social class . . .

Despite obvious improvements since his time, Tawney's analysis remains persuasive. In crucial respects Britain has changed less than it likes to think. Today the passage cited above reads as a reproof to Labour and the Conservatives alike. Socialists in particular should remember that Tawney was by no means an exponent of egalitarianism in education – a much more recent and more nefarious Labour tradition. His solution to the problem of private schools was not to abolish them, but to license them on condition that they accepted bright pupils from all classes, and opened themselves to all able to benefit.

When it comes to independent education, 'old' Labour are as much slaves of inert thinking as the Tories. Both are out of touch with the popular mood. The public is increasingly impatient with the outdated shibboleths of this or that party, being more concerned with common sense. If offered the choice: 'Do you want to leave the private school system as it is, or would you prefer to open it to all, even if this involved selection?' it seems clear that large swathes of the electorate – Conservative, Liberal Democrat and Labour – would go for change, on the simple principle that they had nothing to lose and much to gain.

Private Schools Are the Genuine Comprehensives

At its simplest, the Conservative position on private education consists of taking an absolute stand on choice and individual freedom and refusing to think about anything else. This amounts to saying: 'I insist on exercising my right, as specified in the Universal Declaration of Human Rights 'Parents have a prior right to choose the kind of education that should be given to their children'. Others – for whom I have the greatest sympathy but limited responsibility – must shift for themselves.' When forced on to the defensive such people fall back on more subtle strategies. Typically they will stress that independent schools are attended by children of more varied social backgrounds than in the past, due to scholarships, bursaries, and the great benefactions of the APS. Therefore nothing need change.

Pushed further on to the defensive they will claim, with a straight face, that private schools are the true realisation of the comprehensive ideal. By that they mean that independent schools are not and should not be academically selective institutions. According to this thinking, the rubbing of shoulders between the clever children of the rich and not-so-rich (for example, those with scholarships) on one hand, and the not very clever children of the rich on the other, provides the very things the comprehensives have striven for and failed to attain: a social mix, high academic results, and respect for non-academic achievement. This last factor is normally defined as 'character' – a quality, it appears, confined to the not very clever products of private schools, and inimitable elsewhere.

The ingenuity of the defence must be commended; where

self-interest and social privilege are at stake resourcefulness in argument knows no limits. In its breath-taking irrationality the claim that 'private schools are the true comprehensives' recalls a recent defence of the hereditary right of peers to sit in the House of Lords. Produced by a cross-section of members, it is a classic of its type. Were this right to be threatened, they insist, in delightfully mock-Baroque language:

> Gone would be the young peers of succession, with their distinctive contribution. Gone, we fear, would be the wider sympathies of the House – the product of the arbitrary operation of the hereditary principle – and its capacity to espouse unusual causes, to express attitudes learned in a wide range of ordinary life, and, on occasion, to act as the small boy in the crowd who points out that the emperor has no clothes.

The fact that the arbitrary principle could operate with equal efficiency by rounding up the customers of the nearest pub and decking them in ermine appears to have escaped their Lordships. Ordinary people can be full of useful experience of ordinary life. Some would certainly be quirky enough to espouse in the Upper Chamber the unusual causes they have bored us with in the bar, others quite capable of calling attention to the emperor's lack of clothes.

As that astringent critic of English social mores James McNeill Whistler once remarked: 'The English conceal emptiness with insolence.' To claim that private schools are the true comprehensives, like claiming that the House of Lords is the repository of wisdom about ordinary life, is insolence of a high order, and betrays the emptiness of the educational philosophies of those who resort to this defence. Nevertheless the argument is sincerely held, and in terms of English attitudes to education, highly revealing.

What it shows is that opposition to selection on grounds of ability is no monopoly of socialists, but a cross-party trait. Labour do not want it in comprehensives and Conservatives do not want it in their private schools. Their thinking is of course driven by different concerns: Labour favours conformity, while Conservatives have a raw fear of their places at the best schools in the country being taken by youngsters cleverer than their own.

Though the motives appear opposite, the results are the same, and their effects on our education complementary. Neither left-wing socialists nor old-fashioned Conservatives were ever enthusiastic about grammar schools. This is because neither is happy about anything resembling a meritocracy in education, and neither would be much interested in any reform of private schools that, involving selection as it necessarily would, might tend to bring this about.

What brings politicians of the Left and the Right together is frequently more revealing than what divides them. Political cultures have to spring from somewhere, and this *de facto* concordance of views on schools policy tells us much about the source of our national problems on education. The first is the prevalence in much of our thinking of sentimentalism. The left-wing doctrines of 'progressive education' owe as much to the heart as to the head; similarly on the Right, where sentiment takes the more obviously self-interested form of nostalgia, as much for 'the old school' as for the old ways.

Being romantics at heart, despite their contrasting politics such people often share a gut suspicion of what they see as intellectualism, and hence of selection by ability. The average comprehensive schoolchild may not have much to show in the way of formal education but he or she will be a perfect 'classless' product, a sort of new model person whose most praiseworthy attribute is their very lack of distinction. In the same way the low-achieving public schoolboy, with his healthy contempt for brains, is frequently lauded for his 'strength of character'.

The third factor linking traditionalists of the Left and Right is insularity. The Little Englanderism that unites 'old' Labour and the Europhobe Tories reflects a romantic defiance of the outside world by a shrinking nation. Aspects of this nationalism can be seen in education. Resistance to international comparisons is strong in the education unions and on the Left, except where they can be used to bolster pleas for more resources. Contrasts between teaching methods and results at home and abroad are not welcome, and foreign philosophies and practices are caricatured to escape unflattering comparisons, for example, by mocking the earnestness of the Germans or the uniformity of the French.

The Right, for their part, are more ready to contrast levels of achievement in state schools abroad with those at home to score their party points. Yet the same people are unwilling to reflect on the ultimate sources of our poor national performance, and on what distinguishes our system from those of other countries: its segregated culture. In the eyes of their separate defenders, comprehensives and private schools, however disastrous in combination, are evidence of British distinctiveness and hence, in a strange way, of British superiority: 'We are not as other men are'. In both cases their recipe for the future is the same: do nothing.

Traditionalists of the Left and Right, in education as on Europe, resemble a pair of nervous rabbits. Sensing change in the air they prick up their ears, sniff the wind – and make a bolt for the same hole.

What Is Proposed is Merely a Disguised Form of Nationalisation

It is inevitable that a proposal for a new status for private education will be dubbed 'backdoor nationalisation' on the Right. The poverty of our vocabularies is part of the problem: the conventional political imagination cannot conceive of something beyond its experience, and falls back on simple labels. The charge of 'nationalisation' is unpersuasive. The word carries coercive overtones, whereas the essence of the scheme is that nothing would be done that was not voluntary. If existing private schools chose to remain private, private they would remain to all eternity, and individuals would retain the right to set up as many new schools as they thought the market would bear.

A more justified fear would be a loss of distinctiveness in the schools in question. Yet the Open Sector need not be subjected to the homogenising pressures associated with most forms of state or quasi-state enterprises. The right to autonomy of each school could be spelt out in its statutes, whether this involved teaching methods or traditions. There are precedents for this autonomy: when they were open to state pupils the direct grant schools had no difficulty maintaining their individual ethos.

Aside from the stipulation that pupils be selected by aptitude and ability, and a 'light-touch' financial and academic inspection (for which there is a precedent in the APS) there need be no change in the regime of the new sector. As for the National Curriculum, private schools already shadow this for the most part, and there would be no need to impose it, though schools could adopt a version of it if they wished.

Far from promoting uniformity in the system the addition of formerly private schools, each with its character and traditions, to the gamut of establishments open to all would militate against it. Alongside the thousand or so grant-maintained schools, the 153 existing grammar schools, the sprinking of city technology colleges, and specialist schools of all descriptions, the Open Sector would expand choice for the non-fee-paying public. The result would be an internal market whose dynamism choice, competition and 'best practice' would help to ensure: a world away from any notions of nationalisation in the old sense of the word.

Private Schools Are a Bastion Against a Grey Meritocracy

The thought of their *alma mater* opening its doors to hordes of meritocrats will chill the heart of many an ex-public schoolboy. The analogy with country houses taken over by the National Trust and revealed to the dull incomprehending gaze of day-trippers and picnickers would spring naturally to their minds: the triumph of the public over the private, the death of individualism, the apotheosis of classlessness. Viewed that way, for once it is possible to sympathise with the romantics and sentimentalists, however high the quotient of self-interest.

Yet such analogies would be false. The conversion of a country house into a spectacle for sightseers is a denaturing: something as essentially private as a home has been put on public display and, transformed into a cold, dead cultural artefact, has ceased to be itself. But schools are not dead places, and a private school thrown open to all the talents could well become livelier than before: aerated, as it were, intellectually and socially.

There is a danger in such discussions of forgetting what has been going on in private schools for many years. To a great extent the barbarians are already within the gates. Independent schools have become steadily more academically selective, albeit within their small pool of recruitment, and as has been noted, more than half their pupils come from families with no tradition of private education. The sons and daughters of solicitors, accountants and smallish businessmen are hardly the stuff of *Brideshead Revisited*.

A further objection might be that, as brains became more important than privilege as a test of fitness to enter our best schools, the result would be to replace social by intellectual snobbery. If that is the choice of evils a change of culture might not be such a bad thing; despite some advances, we still suffer more from the former than from the latter, and social snobbishness will not get Britain far in the world of the future.

What would indeed be a disaster, would be if the opening of private schools to all were to prove another step on the desolate road to classlessness. The single most striking aspect of Britain is no longer a readiness to bow the knee to authority and privilege – though the instinct still lingers. Today a new and more pervasive form of deference afflicts us: deference to mediocrity. The most homogenising system of public education in Europe has done its work. In our political as in our cultural life, ordinariness has become a badge of distinction. Everything, of course, has been done in the sacred name of a classless society. But 'classlessness' merely perpetuates the English malaise in another guise. For what is 'classlessness', in England, but class-consciousness, inverted?

Opening private schools to all on the basis of selection (there being no other basis on offer) would go in the opposite direction.

Far from levelling and flattening it would accentuate and reward distinction, wherever it is found. And if it tended to erode posturing and pretension of the proletarian as well as the snobbish variety, so much the better. The sight of an Englishman being himself, all acting aside and free from social inhibitions, would be a fascinating spectacle.

Since There Is Little Prospect of Either the Labour or Conservative Parties Adopting the Proposal in Present Circumstances, What Is the Point of Discussing It?

It is a commonplace of the times that Parliament, frozen in its rhetorical stances and antique animosities, has ceased to be the forum for serious, open-minded debate. The approach of an election is unlikely to encourage free thinking. Yet whether or not an issue is discussed in Party pamphlets or in the Chamber is no indication of its importance to the country. One could almost claim the opposite: that the more important the issue, the less likely it is to be discussed.

The future of the monarchy, the constitution, the long-term financing of the NHS or of social security, and Britain's dangerous over-reliance on the export of arms, are obvious examples. Is society to close its eyes to such matters, simply because our political parties, keener to confront each other than the problems which face the nation, find it mutually inconvenient to debate them? It may indeed be improbable that either Labour or the Conservatives will square up to the problem posed by private education in the near future. The Conservatives in particular seem unlikely to do anything that might progressively erode, as they would see it, the basis of 'their' schools.

Should Tony Blair become Prime Minister there could be a more powerful parliamentary constituency for change. He has referred to himself as a radical of the centre. If he wished to leave his mark on the country, rather than run the danger of being seen by historians as someone who had sought and failed to implement Toryism without the Tories, education would be a natural area for radical thinking of a kind that would go to the centre of the country's problems. If his majority were too small, and 'old Labour' too prominent within it, and the Liberal Democrats failed to back him, then the chances of progress would be minimal. Reform might then have to await the fracturing and reconfiguration of our political parties. With the gulf between Blair and his backbenchers as wide as it is, and the Conservatives as intent as they seem on a schism over Europe, that day may not be as far away as it once appeared.

Meanwhile evasion and procrastination will continue, as successive governments struggle to do what no country has done: construct a first-class system of public education in the absence of any interest or assistance from the most powerful of its citizens. One might just as well seek to design a chicken without a head.

PART TWO

Working from Both Ends

HOW STATE SCHOOLS CAN BE IMPROVED WHILE PRIVATE SCHOOLS ARE OPENED

CHAPTER FIVE

An Instructive Fantasy

Wyndham Lewis and T. E. Hulme, caught short in the street at night, stopped to piss. To a constable who asked what they were doing Hulme replied: 'Do you realise that we are members of the English middle classes?'

'Beg pardon, Sir,' said the constable, and went his way.

* * *

In his influential work *A Theory of Justice*, John Rawls employs an eye-catching device. He asks us to imagine what would happen if everything were returned to the 'original position', and a group of reasonable people, without preconceptions of any kind, were to meet behind a veil of ignorance curtaining off history. Their mandate would be to re-organise society from scratch.

It is tempting to apply the same trick to education: how would we order things, ideally, if we could begin again from the beginning? The weakness of Rawls's device is of course that while history does exist abstract people do not. When you invent them, you tend to put your own thoughts into their minds. In education particularly, the search for reasonable people without preconceptions would be a long one. Nevertheless the temptation is too strong to resist. In our case we do not need to revert to the beginnings of time: we can conduct a more viable experiment while rooting ourselves more firmly than Rawls in current reality.

Picture what would happen if, one otherwise fine morning, the top 7 per cent of society woke up to find that private schools were no longer there: that they had vanished, with all their uniforms and escutcheons and playing fields and jolly dorms, from the face of the Earth. The flippant will say that the first gain would be to literature: what could be more beneficial to our writing than an end to that most narrowly English and clammily introverted of genres, the boarding-school memoir? Others might say that no imagination is necessary to visualise how parents, deprived of their escape routes from state education, would behave.

So imagine a second improbable circumstance: that the ports were sealed, with immigration officials under instructions to apply the same rigour to keeping the British in as to keeping foreigners out. The officials would be ordered to maintain a special watch for overloaded Volvos and BMWs and Mercedes and Jaguars containing agitated-looking couples accompagnied by dejected children answering to names like Harriet and Toby.

'Sorry, the port's closed,' they would say firmly but courteously. 'Welcome to your own country,' some might add with a sardonic smile, arms pointing imperiously up the Dover Road.

Harriet and Toby in the same schools as Jason and Tracy . . . How would our 7 per cent – including as they do a disproportionate number of the movers and shakers of society – react? There seems little doubt; they would move and shake as never before. Indignation would inflate them till they assumed the proportions of wrathful gods. Knowing the power of the upper middle classes, they would waste no time lamenting their fate. There would be instant action. Overnight the 7 per cent would form a Committee for the Improvement of State Education.

Its members would be meticulously chosen: seven wise men and women, comprising one judge, one vice-chancellor, a scientist, an engineer, an arts person, a headteacher of a private day school, and a businessman/accountant. Its timespan of action would be that of the Almighty – seven days; where the education of their children was concerned our Gods would be in a hurry. In the space of a single week the Seven-per-cent Committee, endowed with supernatural powers, would do the impossible: restructure a system of education to which they had hitherto given scarcely a moment's thought.

Being intelligent folk they would go straight to the source of the problem, bypassing institutions from which little was to be hoped. Which is to say that they would ignore Parliament. Scornful of a political process that had allowed things to get to the state they were, our middle-class Gods would cast aside democratic scruple and resort to direct action.

Day One would be devoted to a reform of the reigning philosophy of education. This involved brief and purgative visits to the educational institutes and teacher training establishments. The university authorities sheltering them under their wings, more from habit than necessity, proved only too anxious to oblige. Nervous of accusations of political interference, previously they had had little to do with educational studies. Now, however, things had changed.

Having no refuge for their children in the private sector any more than the visiting Committee itself, and realising that if state schools did not improve dramatically the quality of their universities would be in question, the authorities co-operated energetically in the *putsch*. Oxbridge academics – strangely reticent about the deficiencies of state schools till now – volunteered in droves, together with some of the most distinguished minds in the country, to work on the Royal Commission on teacher training our Committee set up on the spot: report to be delivered by 9.30 the following morning.

By noon on the Second Day a new educational philosophy had been adopted. It had been a hard morning's work. The Committee were as unfamiliar as they were impatient with the opaque theorising and tortuousness of expression characteristic of every document set before them. The new principles guiding state education were arrived at swiftly and by novel procedures. First, surplus language was stripped away from the writings of educationalists and bureaucrats to see what was left. What was left was an immoveable conviction that schools should be as near-identical as possible, to suit the ideology of the educationalists and the convenience of the bureaucrats.

Next, the Committee pulled a neat trick. By simply reversing these attitudes and assumptions a working philosophy of education was established: schools should be as diverse as possible and bureaucracy shaved to a minimum. As for teaching methods, at the stroke of a pen minds were cleansed of egalitarian dogma. As for parental involvement, there would be 'as much as seemed desirable'. The Committee in its wisdom had no illusions that parents were necessarily the best people to run schools, any more than patients were the best people to run hospitals. They themselves had never had to interfere overmuch in their independent schools, content in the main to consign the education of their children to people whose profession it was to accomplish it.

The remainder of the Second Day was spent at work on the system. Composed as it was of commonsensical people, the Committee did what no British Government has done in recent memory: they began at the beginning. Which is to say that they called for papers on nursery education. Studies were at once produced from dusty shelves, showing that infants who began school at three had a head-start over the others for the rest of their education, nay for their natural lives. These yellowing bales of paper the Committee brushed rudely aside. Had they not spent thousands of pounds annually on pre-prep schools for their own children, without sweating over page after page of the groaningly obvious?

So it was that, early in the evening of the Second Day, the Committee issued its first decree: nursery schools were to be established for all from the age of three. Doors to open at 8.30 next morning, not least for the convenience of the members of the Committee and their spouses, all of them professional men and women. Days of enforced idleness by high-earning ladies were in danger of stretching family finances, and disputes about who should mind the children were stretching family nerves. Despite this haste the Committee was careful to stipulate that the quality of early learning they had enjoyed in the private sector be made available to all. Funds for these expensive educational accessories would be withdrawn instantly if they turned out to be no more than glorified play-groups.

On the morning of the Third Day the Committee, warming to

its task and flattered by the public acclamation that had followed the announcement of new nurseries, turned its attention to primary schools. Lightning visits to a number of typical establishments confirmed the truth of headlines they dimly recalled seeing in the national press – dimly because, with their own children elsewhere at the time, they had had no incentive to linger over distressing reports detailing what was happening to the rest. Now that nurseries had been established far more could be expected of education from five to eleven. Henceforth primary schools would blossom, not least because the brisk overhauling of the teaching profession had done away with its footling and wrongheaded philosophies.

The same principle of escalating expectations was applied at secondary level, dealt with on Day Four. Here the Committee hesitated briefly, as papers even more voluminous than those on nursery education were circulated dealing with that most intractable of issues, selection. In a short discussion, decades of pointless debate between Left and Right were brushed aside. To the Committee such people seemed intent on re-fighting obsolete class wars: a pastime well suited to educationalists or Parliamentarians but for which busy and intelligent people had neither time nor appetite.

A full-scale return to the grammar school/secondary modern pattern was ruled briskly out of court, for three reasons:

(1) no one wanted a system that had failed the majority.
(2) the term ‘selection by ability’ was in any case outdated. What mattered nowadays was aptitude and motivation, plus a high level of aspiration, especially in maths, science and technological studies.
(3) the Committee members did not fancy sending their own children to low-aiming, low-achieving secondary schools with facilities to match, should they inexplicably fail the eleven-plus examination.

In much the same way old-style comprehensives, with their dubious teaching methods and levelling effects, were ruled out. Perfectly tolerable for the 93 per cent in the old days (the arts person confessed, with a twinge of shame, how she had argued over many a dinner table that comprehensives were 'marvellous in principle') such places were no longer tolerable now. As for the argument that comprehensives would flourish if only people like themselves sent their children there, the Committee dismissed that in an instant. As the ex-private headmistress, a frosty lady made frostier by the unaccountable disappearance of her school, remarked: 'Discriminating parents of whatever background do not send their children to school to be socially engineered, but for purposes of education.'

A search for a solution to the structure of our schools lighted swiftly on something approaching the German model – a model, it was explained to the Committee, that the British themselves had helped to set up during the post-war occupation. The main advantage was that high-quality technological education would be available for those for whom it was appropriate. Such schools, it was subsequently decreed, were to be particularly well resourced, not simply because of demands for computers and the like, but because a great effort was needed to raise the standing of technological education in a country where it has never enjoyed the prestige it had abroad. It was further noted that the presence of children from the privileged classes in specialist technological schools would do wonders for their reputation, as for the quality of the teachers employed.

Worries about undue emphasis on vocational subjects expressed by the vice-chancellor (a classics man) and the arts person were silenced when it was explained to them that high aspirations in the humanities depended directly on equally high ambitions in science and technology. One validated the other. Specialist schools in technology meant that others could specialise in more academic pursuits without those outmoded words 'privilege' or 'elitism' – depressingly familiar in the old private school days – entering the picture.

Lumping everything together, as had too frequently been done in the past, risked reducing everything to a mush. Now that there was no need to keep levels of achievement down to avoid any impression of one child being more gifted or assiduous than another, the humanities curriculum could be upgraded accordingly. Latin, the vice-chancellor was quick to point out, could henceforth be made available for all likely to profit from it. The Committee acquiesced, while stressing that priority would be given to rather more recent languages.

Newcomer to the field of education as he was, not even the businessman was so simple-minded as to wish for science not to be studied by academic pupils, or for languages or literature to be excluded from largely technological courses. Allowance was also made for the possibility of late-developers switching from one school or course to another.

Day Five was reserved for a look at national testing, teachers' pay, and examination structure. National testing, it was swiftly agreed, would henceforth be abolished. So far as the Committee could ascertain the entire cumbrous system had been established more to check up on the professionalism of the teachers than on the achievement of the pupils – the latter being determined to a large extent by the former. Now that the profession had been reformed at the roots, more sensible attitudes would prevail.

Teachers would test their pupils automatically, as had been done without fuss in the sadly defunct private sector. For the state to continue to look over their shoulders would be an insult to a freshly galvanised and newly respected profession. The businessman noted with satisfaction that millions of pounds would be saved on time-wasting, centrally administered tests.

Teachers' pay was dealt with at some length, which is to say an hour. On one hand it was pointed out that teachers in the private sector had been paid approximately the same as in the state sector. On the other, that they were doing a somewhat different job: instructing the young at Eton or Westminster or Winchester was a quite different proposition from encouraging respect for higher cultural values at Moss Side or Bethnal Green. As the businessman put it, with charming bluntness: 'Get it wrong at Winchester and the worst that could happen would be the loss of an Oxbridge place. Get it wrong at Moss Side and society has one more criminal on its hands.'

For the first time in the Committee's proceedings there was

stalemate: three against three with the businessman having the casting vote. Everyone watched to see which way he would go. For some moments he was all confusion. Tempted initially to pay as little as he could get away with, he finally came to a directly opposite conclusion: 'We've got to recruit the best available, which means we have to have enough applicants lined up to turn people away. A more professional profession deserves more professional pay.'

Swung by this happy phrase, the Committee decided unanimously on an across the board rise of 10 per cent – with improved differentials for headteachers, and teachers of maths, science and technology. The increase was to be backdated to the day of the disappeared private schools (a small and inexpensive gesture, though their hearts were in it).

The long-vexed question of A-levels was dispatched in a matter of minutes. Businessman, arts person, scientist and engineer – all agreed instantly that they were too narrow. Children today needed to have some knowledge of science if they are arts-oriented, and vice versa. That was what modernity was about. Henceforth five subjects were to be studied, in sensible combinations, with minimal loss of breadth in each subject and *absolutely no loss of intellectual rigour.* [Italics added by the vice-chancellor and the headmistress.]

The reason A-levels had not been reformed earlier, it was noted in the Committee minutes, was the fear that the educational establishment would turn the reform to their advantage. With its non-educational agenda and lingering distrust of any formal examinations at all, it might well have seized the opportunity to lower expectations across the board, to minimise competition and ensure that everyone qualified for higher education.

In this connection there was unanimous support for the view that the most extraordinary care would henceforth need to be taken to prevent any dilution of standards for the children of the most demanding people in society, which is to say themselves. At one point the businessman became somewhat carried away on the point. Enthusing about how high standards at the top would henceforth communicate themselves to the bottom, he let slip the phrase 'trickle-down effect'. The metaphor being thought a little too gross, and somewhat condescending, the businessman did not pursue it, though it was clear from the smiles of his colleagues that, not for the first time, the bluff-spoken fellow had hit the nail squarely on the head.

Finally the Committee turned to higher education. Till recently the universities had been in better shape than the schools, in consequence of their selective ethos and mode of entry. Yet here too they found signs of decline, due mainly to the suddenness of expansion. The overnight improvement in the performance of the schools would, the Committee was confident, help to sustain quality. 'Get it right at the bottom and it'll come right at the top' was the businessman's sagacious comment.

There followed a brief tug of war between the scientist, the engineer and the businessman on one hand, and the vice-chancellor, headmistress and arts person on the other (the judge havering judiciously in the middle) on the question of the disproportionate number of arts graduates produced by our institutions of higher learning. Finally it was recognised by all that there was indeed something amiss. It was agreed to take measures to tip the balance the other way, to satisfy the demands of the economy, while ensuring that degrees in arts subjects were made somewhat more demanding.

Conscious that reforms in the schools would enable underused talent to rise from lowly social places, with the risk that competition could increase to the point where their own children might not coast quite so easily into the finest universities in the land, the Committee took a sympathetic look at the finances and facilities of the less prestigious institutions. These included the former polytechnics, where a higher proportion of children with similar backgrounds to their own might find themselves in future. Despite the press of time, such was the level of interest that a site visit was deemed necessary.

Having never frequented such places in the flesh, the Committee were appalled by the sight of overcrowded libraries and lecture rooms, and saddened by the almost complete lack of tutorial attention they had enjoyed at their own much-cherished *alma maters*. Fearing the consequences for the worth of their children's degrees, not to speak of those of other people's, and knowing that money of the order required would not be forthcoming from any government, the Committee decreed that a graduate tax for fees as well as maintenance come into force the following day. It was observed that public acclaim was more muted than in the case of the new nurseries.

On the Sixth Day the Committee charged their businessman/ accountant with the task of estimating the cost of what they had created. At the outset of the affair he had suggested fixing a budget, but had been over-ruled. To do so, it was passionately objected, would have been to prejudge the discussion, forcing the Committee to cram a new dispensation in state education into an arbitrary financial framework. To say that when it came to education money was no object would be to exaggerate the Committee's view. But they came damn close to it. As former fee-payers themselves they were only too aware that parents would sacrifice anything for the future of their children. The same was surely the case, the vice-chancellor opined loftily, for the future of the country.

Persuading the public of the need for offsetting reductions in less urgent areas of expenditure proved surprisingly easy. As the businessman intoned magisterially (he had caught the committee style) in the course of a nation-wide broadcast announcing their unanimous conclusions: 'If we can't afford education we can't afford an economy, or a civilised culture.'

On the Seventh Day the Committee rested from its labours. Contemplating the reaction to their work on TV and in the press they agreed that, overall, it was pretty good.

Chapter Six

Nursery Schools

'I got it! Why don't we try a combination of all the ingredients?'

(Line spoken by a scientist in a spectacularly bad science fiction film)

* * *

There are times when it is possible to wonder how serious the English are about education. On some occasion during the half-century since the Second World War one might have expected that we would rethink things from the beginning, in the light of the limitations and failings of the 1944 Education Act. No government ever has. The absence of any logical order in our reforms over five decades has been the most striking thing about them. We did secondary schools before primaries (comprehensives in 1965, primaries in the Plowden report of 1967), and the end of the educational process (the expansion of higher education in the sixties and late eighties) before the beginning (nursery schools). Technical and vocational education we began to get round to, piecemeal, after four decades of failure. In our education planning, as at Heathrow Airport, we add bits on as we go along. And we still haven't got to the beginning.

Nursery education, one might have thought, would have been seized on instantly, not just for itself but as a way of evening up the unequal chances that characterise the system; and as part of the solution to the problem of broken homes and juvenile delinquency which are becoming a particular British phenomenon. Yet at the end of the twentieth century we are still arguing about whether or not early learning should be a priority, whether we can afford it, and how it should be done.

An amateur educationalist might conclude, after a moment's reflection, that early learning might allow primary schools to hoist their expectations, secondary schools to build on surer foundations, and so on up the line. He might also suspect that a child trained in basic social disciplines from the age of three might turn out to have fewer problems in later life. Unsurprisingly such have been the conclusions of numerous reports over a long period, notably a study by an American, Berrueta-Clement, in 1984 (*Changed Lives: Monographs of the High*, Scope Educational Research Foundation).

Nursery school pupils not only did better throughout their school years and professional lives; they were also less likely to have behavioural problems, to be arrested by the police, to take drugs, or to have teenage pregnancies. Berrueta-Clement also demonstrated what might be thought to be another self-evident fact by showing that money spent on early education was easily recouped by savings on the treatment of delinquents, social security payments, etc. In Britain of the nineties the advantages of getting three-year-old children away from fractured homes in inner cities into a secure, purposeful environment, if only for a few hours a day, seem self-evident.

There is no doubt about the popularity of nursery education, notably amongst the middle classes, and consequently no lack of verbal commitments by successive governments. For more than a quarter of a century, beginning with Mrs Thatcher as Education Secretary in 1970, we have been circling round the subject. On early learning governments have been strong on pious definitions of the aims and weak when it came to supplying the means. Both parties have shifty records.

In 1972 Mrs Thatcher's White Paper extolled the virtues of an early start and promised nursery places for all three- and four-year-olds. Labour too made positive noises during its subsequent period in office, yet little was done. By the late eighties we had circled back to the beginning of the seventies. Thoughtful documents were produced extolling virtues already extolled. First came a 1989 House of Commons Select Committee Report: 'We conclude from the evidence that education for under-fives can effectively contribute to the various social, educational and compensatory objectives set out in the 1972 White Paper.' Then came the Rumbold Report of the Department of Education and Science (DES) in 1990: 'Attitude and behaviour patterns established during the first years of life are central to future educational and social learning.' In nursery education, incantation has taken over from action. We offer up our prayers, feel better about ourselves, and continue our sins of omission as before.

The international statistics thrust in the face of the Government and the public by the early learning lobby are equally familiar. The figures are startling: in France, Germany and Italy 75–95 per cent of three- and four-year-olds are in publicly funded childcare: in Britain around 40 per cent. By way of compensation the Government claims that 'Diversity is the hallmark of pre-school provision for the under-fives in England.' So we are reduced, somewhat pathetically, to putting the best gloss we can on inadequate provision. (Could it be that our primaries, some of which resemble nothing so much as nurseries, are run by frustrated nursery teachers?)

One man's 'diversity' is another man's rag-bag. Instead of structured education we have nursery classes, nursery units in primary schools, pre-school playgroups, child-minding – everything except the thing itself. A few years ago a mere 8 per cent of English children enjoyed the benefits of serious, structured, full-time nursery schools: 4 per cent in the private sector, and 4 per cent in the public; another statistic that speaks for itself.

The consensus on the undoubted benefits of nursery schools makes our collective failure to act intriguing. Explanations are called for which go beyond the usual ones of procrastination and shortage of money. The first thing that seems to distinguish us from others are our high levels of tolerance where education is concerned – or as Aneurin Bevan famously put it, the poverty of aspiration of the British working classes. In other countries nurseries are seen as a necessity, in Britain as a luxury.

An element of social status may well be involved. In Britain a good education is associated with class to a far greater degree than abroad. In their unquestioning, deferential way, millions of parents, under-educated themselves, appear to see serious nursery education, like good schools, as something highly desirable to those who can afford them, but not for them. The same people who dissolve in pools of patriotic sentimentality over photographs of this or that princess dropping off her three-year-old princeling at his private nursery are, when it comes to their own children and their needs, strangely undemanding. If they were to ask why their children could not enjoy the same advantages as people in high places they would be accused of envy, and marked down as covert republicans.

Our poor performance on nursery education is another example of the price we pay for our culture of separate development. Provision varies greatly from one LEA to another, but many at the bottom are obliged to make do with what they are given – play groups, reception classes, childminding arrangements, whatever surrogates are deemed appropriate for people of their condition. Those who are able to buy high-quality nursery schooling do so as a matter of course, thereby reinforcing the educational advantage enjoyed by their children, and entrenching the great divide from the age of three.

To escape state primary schools, the better-off send their children to prep schools. To escape comprehensives, they go to independent secondary schools. And now, should the voucher scheme be generally adopted, more and more will be able to attend private nurseries to escape the state equivalent. In education, it seems, even more than elsewhere, to those who have, it shall be given.

Another explanation for the hesitations and broken promises of governments of all stripes may be an underlying lack of confidence in the educational establishment. Even the Labour Party might quail at the implications of a full-blown national education service, with all its potential for organisational and doctrinal disputation.

The idea of setting up a new, universal tier of education from the age of three to five, with the never-ending demands that would inevitably follow (for more resources, more training, more research, more psychiatrists, more special provision, better facilities and so on), pursued by highly unionised teachers exploiting public anxieties about the state of our infant schools, promises an administrative nightmare. Politicians of all inclinations would be quick to spot the risk of establishing a money-eating machine, with 'expert' insistence that only such and such a ratio of teachers and toilets per class was remotely tolerable.

From a Conservative perspective, the nightmare worsens. Nursery advocates insist heavily on the need for professionally trained staff. Who would do the training, and according to which theories? Would not LEAs convert nurseries into social laboratories, with the emphasis less on preparing the child for formal learning than on preparing it for the 'comprehensive ideal', as they have already done with primaries? And at the end of it all there would be no guarantee of quality. To spend almost a billion pounds annually on running a smart new nursery machine complete with 'marvellous facilities', but dispensing pre-school education on an only marginally superior level to that which children would receive from childminders or at play groups, would be yet another 'great British educational disaster'.

The fears may seem all too rational, yet the logical conclusion – that the educational profession cannot be trusted to run an efficient, high-quality service – is unacceptable. The implication that in countries with different social traditions, whose educational head is not severed from its body, these things are possible, but that in Britain it is hopeless, would be an appalling admission of defeat.

At present something is finally being done. This time the extension being tacked on to our educational Heathrow Airport in late response to growing demand takes the form of a voucher system for early schooling. The structure has a tentative, experimental look about it, the design an air of compromise. Its ambitions are limited: it is not aimed at housing three-to-five but only four-year-olds. It involves little new money (£165 million), much of the cost coming from recycling resources between existing state and private schools.

For good reasons and bad the majority of local authorities have said they will have nothing to do with the experiment. It is rumoured on good authority that originally the Secretary of State for Education, Gillian Shephard, wanted nothing to do with it either, and that its tentative, spatchcocked nature was due to the determination of marketeers in the Cabinet to conduct a voucher experiment in education somewhere, somehow. So it is that, while other European countries have proven systems of nursery education for children of three and over, Britain tinkers with a voucher scheme involving a limited number of children at small cost, and based on a system that, where it has been tried, has been shown to produce dubious results.

The merits or otherwise of the voucher scheme will emerge in practice. Whatever happens it will increase the net amount of nursery education available, which will be something. What seems clear in advance is that a voucher system will risk producing the perverse effects discussed in Chapter 3 ('Bogus Solutions'). Every parent will receive the £1,100 pounds voucher annually, irrespective of wealth. In resisting demands for full-scale nursery provision the Government has often taken the line that it would be too expensive: yet the first effect of the voucher scheme will be to hand out money to those who have shown themselves willing and able to pay private fees. Since there will be no attempt to recoup a portion of that money through taxation, in redistributive terms, the effect will be to compound the anomaly whereby well-to-do mothers receive the same child benefit as everyone else.

More significant from the standpoint of the theme of this book, middle-income parents who have hitherto been unable to afford fees at a private nursery will in many cases be able to top up their £1,100 with whatever is necessary to escape from the state system – as many most certainly would if they received a similar voucher for secondary education. Money raised in taxes from people who may be poorer than themselves will be invested in new or existing private nurseries, likely to remain beyond the reach of the average parent.

The point is not to decry the choice of rich parents to resort to private nurseries, many of which may be of a superior standard. The problem is one of equity. The most likely result of the experiment in nursery education will be the opposite of what the Government intended. Instead of providing choice for everyone, it will extend it for the few. The Government will respond that there is no reason why LEAs should not provide a service of equivalent quality, yet there is.

By their nature many (though by no means all – there are some do-it-yourself establishments) private nurseries are more likely to have superior premises and smaller classes. For obvious social reasons they are less likely to have to deal with difficult or disruptive pupils. Most important, like private schools in general, private nurseries will tend to be patronised by parents whose vigilance about standards does not extend to state provision. The schools will therefore tend to enjoy a standing advantage over public provision, being less likely to fall prey to quasi-political doctrines and dubious theories of education than their state equivalents. It is significant that, even before the voucher experiment was introduced, nursery education was one of the fastest-expanding areas in the private sector in 1995 (ISIS, Annual Census Report, 1996).

Yet again we come back to our blocked society. The bigger the private sector grows – in this case assisted directly by taxpayers' cash – the less incentive there will be for the powerful and affluent to take an enlightened interest in the quality of state provision. In nursery education as elsewhere the vicious circle seems destined to spin on as before

Nothing illustrates our lack of will and common endeavour as vivdly as our blinkeredness and foot-dragging on nursery schools. Here is a single, well-defined area where results are virtually guaranteed, where the cost/benefit analysis speaks for itself, and where current sacrifice in terms of investment would yield almost immediate returns. But in Britain there *is* no sense of common endeavour. One of the results is that we still have no first rung on the educational ladder.

Chapter Seven

Playing at Schools

'There is excellent adult authority for the conviction that for certain moral and intellectual purposes adults must become like little children.'

(John Dewey, Democracy and Education).

* * *

The British are a case to themselves when it comes to theory. From the beginnings of our modern literature we have poked fun at abstract modes of thinking: 'The philosopher teacheth, but he teacheth obscurely, so as only the learned can understand him,' wrote Sir Philip Sidney in his *Defence of Poetry*. The workings of the English mind have been admired by our neighbours, from Voltaire to André Gide: Voltaire compared English thought to a tree spreading its branches naturally, as opposed to the formal garden of French thinking; Gide once contrasted the abstract imperative and floating infinite of '*défense d'afficher*' unfavourably with the mightily solid injunction 'Stick No Bills'.

Yet when it comes to education, this robust pragmatism disappears. The earth-creeping English, with their 'step-by-step' caution and healthy scepticism are carried away by strange doctrines and wild stratagems. The consequences are invariably disastrous. Unused to heady abstractions, we do not know how to handle them. Instead of turning them over this way and that, testing them against practice as we would in any other field of activity, we implement them in our schools with all the doggedness and literal-mindedness at our disposal, which is a lot.

An Englishman with an idea in his head is a dangerous animal: like a borzoi off the leash he streaks away, mouth agape, in the direction in which his nose is pointing. In our pursuit of doctrinal purity we out-do foreigners far more theoretically-minded than ourselves. The comprehensive concept was taken to extremes unknown abroad, and a similar absolutist mentality has gripped the Right in recent years, as it strains to force education into the mould of the market economy

Primary schools are another example of this unnatural propensity to dogma in our thinking on education. Once we got it into our heads that primaries were not really schools in the old-fashioned sense, but cradles of democracy and creativity, there was no stopping us. No one stands in the way of an Englishman with the light of inner virtue streaming from his eye. And for three decades, from the Plowden Report to the damning results of the national tests, few dared.

Primary classes in British schools are a heart-stopping sight. The charm of infants engaged in discovering the universe and its wonders captivates the most hardened sceptic. The impression is one of amiable chaos, of a world re-created by innocents – though the chaos is by no means accidental. As the teachers flit from child to child, doing their distracted best to comfort or cajole each distracted infant, they are working to a theory.

Tell them that they are engaged in the implementation of a rigid and outdated dogma and they would be incredulous. The open-plan classrooms, the children scattered round tables, the buzz and shriek of voices as they practise the 'discovery' and 'self-discovery' ethos – rigid dogma? The whole point of their methods, the teacher would protest, is their informality. Outdated? But it is formal, traditional teaching that is outdated! The teachers are being progressive, and like anyone who has convinced themselves that they have cast off the incubus of the past, they feel exceedingly good about it.

There is a terrible fervour about our attachment to progressive education, characteristic of late converts. A similar attitude is apparent in the English attitude to sex. A sorely inhibited country not so long ago, now our zeal in the cause of liberty – and libertinism – knows no limits. As Philip Larkin observed in a line too famous to quote, you would have thought no one had ever done it before.

The same is true of our approach to abstract art; there too the English are late converts. The Tate Gallery lagged grievously behind its international equivalents in buying contemporary work. One result is a weak collection of modern classics; another is a relentless resolve to display our unshockability, long after everyone else has given up any pretence of being shocked. A century after modernism began, the Tate sets about making up for lost time with an indiscriminate passion for whatever is new. In primary education, it is the same. A century or more after progressive theories were invented the English are implementing them uncritically and with terrible zeal.

The sources of the teaching methods used in our primary schools range from Pestalozzi, Froebel and Piaget to the American philosopher and educationalist John Dewey (1859–1952). Though still thought of as modern, all go back in some degree to the eighteenth-century ideas of Jean-Jacques Rousseau. Teachers undergoing training are rarely conversant with any of these texts. The dangers of inherited doctrines being filtered and fed into uncritical minds need no underlining, especially when the doctrines in question are of an emotive nature. Once lodged in the head and the heart of teachers ill-equipped to question them, they are hard to shift. Young teachers are proud to be acquainted with theory, even if they do not understand that one theory can frequently be negated by another.

One of the more recent and influential of the founding fathers of progressive education was Dewey. Like the free-market guru Milton Friedman, Dewey taught for a time at the Unversity of Chicago. He saw the education of his time as little more than the handing down of sterile concepts to passive children, and derided the 'rows of ugly desks placed in geometrical order . . . the bare walls . . .' Instead of soaking up without question what they were told, he believed children should be encouraged to find out things for themselves, work communally, move around, express themselves, and generally treat the classroom as a 'laboratory' of learning.

The reaction against the dry-as-dust, hierarchical approach to teaching of the nineteenth century was as inevitable as it was in many respects salutary. Few today would not accept many of Dewey's criticisms of traditional methods. In the hands of British educationalists his theories of what should replace them – in many respects highly contestable – have become regurgitated dogma. Compare the following:

> There is very little place in the traditional schoolroom for the child to work. The workshop, the laboratory, the materials, the tools with which the child may construct, create, and actively enquire, and even the requisite space have been for the most part lacking . . . The fallacy consists in believing that one can begin with ready-made subject matter of arithmetic, geography or whatever . . . Education is going on in a one-sided way, for attitudes and habits are in process that stand in the way of the future learning that springs from easy and ready contact and communication with others . . . The child becomes the sun round which the appliances of education revolve: he is the centre around which they are organised.

These excerpts come from Dewey's *School and Society* (1899) and his *Democracy and Education* (1916). Over half a century later the Plowden Report on primary education wrote:

> A school . . . is a community in which children learn to live first and foremost as children and not as future adults . . . The school sets out deliberately to devise the right environment for children to allow them to be themselves and to develop at the pace appropriate to them . . . It lays special stress on individual discovery, on first-hand experience and on opportunities for creative work. It insists that

> knowledge does not fall neatly into separate compartments and that work and play are not opposites but complementary.

In 1993 – now almost a century after *School and Society* – Caroline Gipps, Dean of Research at the London Institute of Education, wrote the following critique of Government policy:

> Current directions in central policy in education are at odds with the directions which research on learning and cognition would tell us to take. The transmission model of teaching, in a traditional formal classroom, with strong subject and task boundaries and traditional narrow assessment, is the opposite of what we need to produce learners who can think critically, synthesize and transform, experiment and create. We need a flexible curriculum, active cooperative forms of learning, opportunities for pupils to talk through the knowledge which they are incorporating, open forms of assessment (e.g. self-evaluation and reflection on their learning); in short a thinking curriculum aimed at higher order performance and cognitive skills.'

Thus are orthodoxies born. Nowhere are they more tenacious than in education, where they stagnate in the closed pool of a highly introverted world. If Deweyism is indeed gospel truth there is no reason why a single word should ever be changed, or a single concept challenged. This seems to be the view of the majority of our educationalists. Not one notion in the Plowden or Gipps passages differs from what Dewey wrote, and much is identical. The deterioration of style common in all mechanically reproduced thinking is evident, as the freshness of the original falls first into the sedateness of an official report, and finally into the ugly and obscure jargon of institutionalised doctrine: 'produce learners'; 'active cooperative forms of learning'; 'the knowledge which they are incorporating'. Deweyism having acquired the status of science, it is decorated with not one but two 'cognitives'.

In thousands of classrooms across the country the theory is put into practice laboriously, and with an intolerant eye. Informality is applied with scientific rigour. No straight rows of desks or chairs are to be seen, as if, like Victorian piano legs, they were an affront to the puritanical conscience. The very schools (open-plan, no closed-off spheres, every room interacting) are constructed to ideological specification. Whole-class teaching has not been scaled back judiciously, for use where appropriate, but virtually abolished: recent studies show that it is down to 15 per cent of the time spent in the classroom, while 77 per cent is spent with pupils working alone (Galten: *Crisis in the Primary Classroom*, 1994).

As for the learning by rote of dates or poetry, it is not simply something that can be overdone: it is the teaching method of the devil. As for grammar, you can bandy about the most intimate parts of the human body as much as you like, but on no account must you allude to the parts of speech.

Deweyism in education is a very American mixture of scientism and sentimentality ('The child becomes the sun around which the appliances of education revolve . . .'). If the results were clearly superior we might worry less about the philosophical origins. But that is not the case. However informal the surroundings, however prettified the walls, however amiably disorganised the 'learning environment', however warm we feel when surveying the children pottering about their little laboratories, in its British manifestation at least, Dewey's beautiful theory has not worked.

It is not only 'educational reactionaries' who say so. In recent years HM Inspectors have been timorously alluding to the risk of low expectations that can go with informal teaching methods, though none except the present Chief Inspector of HMI, Christopher Woodhead, has suggested that there may be something amiss with the old orthodoxy. For years teachers at secondary level have complained that they were obliged to make up ground uncovered in the little Edens of amateur learning our primary schools have become. Middle-class parents especially have become more concerned, and those in a position to do so are increasingly taking a deep breath and escaping to the prep-school sector: between 1985 and 1990 places at private prep schools increased by 12 per cent.

Disquiet about informal teaching methods has spread across the political spectrum. The Labour Party, breaking with a long and culpable tradition of silence, has joined the chorus of critics of low aspirations. David Blunkett has called for a re-examination of 'progressive methods' (speech of 30 May 1996), after seeing the results of the national tests at 7, as well as at 11 and 14.

It is worth reflecting for a moment on the implications of national testing at so young an age. It is hard to be sympathetic to the idea. It is not (or should not be) the British way of doing things. There is something Prussian about it, and centralisation and regimentation are distasteful for whatever purpose.

In a satisfactory system national testing would not be necessary. Teachers would test their pupils formally and informally at regular intervals to discover their progress and take corrective action where necessary, as is done routinely in the best private schools. One might have thought that it was the minimum one might ask of the profession. Yet they cannot be relied upon to do it.

Parliament does not know the educational state of the nation and it does not trust the profession to tell it. Like keeping an entire class in school after hours, national testing is a form of collective punishment. Good and bad teachers know what is happening and are equally indignant, the former with justification, the latter with none. If it were felt that the good vastly outnumbered the bad and the mediocre, as Ministers are obliged to pretend, testing would never have happened, and the Opposition would never have supported it. But that is not the general perception.

It is understandable that it should be done once, as a sort of Domesday survey, to see how we stand. But to make testing a regular feature of the system is a baleful act: an admission not just of past failure, but of failure to come. The possibility that the teachers might be induced to achieve acceptable standards, monitor learning effectively on their own initiative and be helped or fired by their Heads if they do not, is implicitly written off.

Institutionalised testing of schools is the equivalent of ordering an annual survey of the structural soundness of all new buildings constructed by British engineers, or calling in all British-built cars for an annual survey in addition to the MOT. The implication would be that our production techniques were inherently faulty, that routine quality checks were not to be relied on, and that any improvement at source was not a realistic hope.

There is substance in some of the teachers' complaints about the entire procedure, even if they have brought it on their own heads. It is one thing for a seven-year-old to be regularly tested and encouraged on how to do better next time, another to be seen publicly to fall below the accepted standard at such an early age. They are right too to complain about bureaucracy and over-centralisation which – amongst other inherent vices – can breed over-conformity.

Then there is the risk of imposing an arbitrary standard in individual subjects. Will it be too high, or too low? *Quis custodiet ipsos custodes*? Much could depend on different personalities appointed by different governments. Would a Labour Government be less rigorous than a Conservative one? And if the failure rate were too high would even a Conservative Government, worried perhaps for electoral reasons at the disaffection of the teachers, bend in the wind? The very notion of a single fixed grid of achievement covering all stages of a child's development rings alarm bells. Almost everyone is unhappy about it for one reason or another. Nevertheless, such was our uncertainty about how the great experiment in primary education was progressing, that it had to be done, even at seven.

The results justified the concerns. Twenty per cent of seven-year-olds were unable to achieve level two in the test on reading and mathematics. At eleven 52 per cent failed to reach a satisfactory standard in English and mathematics.

The reaction from the Right to the testing exercise was predictable. From the Left, less so. It is here that the change of critical climate has been most noticeable:

> For all the obvious attractions of the discovery methods ('finding out' rather than 'being told') research showed even the best teachers had problems managing different groups of children pursuing different projects within the same classroom. It can waste time, reduce teacher–pupil contact, and make it immensely more difficult to monitor achievement. Worse still, in the words of a former liberal educator, progressive education has persuaded people to 'jump on the bandwagon when they can't play the instruments'.

Taken from a *Guardian* editorial (26 January 1996) – a newspaper widely seen as the house magazine of the teaching and sociological professions – this is a significant statement. Similar criticisms have cropped up with increasing frequency in the editorial columns of the *Observer* and the *Independent*. When such newspapers start banging the same drum as the *Daily Mail* and the *Daily Telegraph*, something is happening.

Whether the educational establishment will take note is another matter. The validity of the tests was questioned by the very same people who proffered excuses for the poor results (if the tests are invalid, why the excuses?) Classroom sizes, inadequate training, shortage of books and facilities, leaking roofs – even the disruption to teaching caused by the tests themselves was cited in defence. Even if all these factors are present, they do not pertain everywhere and do not go to the root problem. There was no indication in the reaction from the teacher unions, the LEAs, or the educationalists that methods based on a hundred-year-old theory and perpetuated in the teacher training establishments for decades may conceivably be in need of re-examination in the light of results.

The findings of the tests were particularly damning in mathematics, where something of a national crisis has developed. For many years teaching styles have moved away from basic arithmetic to concentrate on the new mathematics, whose theory was more congenial to informal teaching practices in primary schools and to the mixed-ability doctrines which, though less widespread than they were, are still in force in some comprehensives. Despite expert criticism of the theory and its demonstrably poor results measured by international standards (see page 158), reluctance to review it has continued. Heads of private schools have noted that entrants from state primaries are roughly two years behind those from prep schools – one reason why some private schools find it hard to accept state school children at all.

If Deweyism – which the philosopher himself described as a Copernican revolution – has scientific status then its workings should be systematically measured against results. Yet the implications of any tests for the validity of the theory have been avoided, as experts content themselves with re-stating the doctrine in different words. The following is an extract from the SEAC in its advice on GCSE maths: '. . . traditionally mathematics has been about knowing the rules to deal with numbers, percentages, equations and so on. It has often been divided into arithmetic, algebra, and geometry . . . One approach here is to let pupils explore their own ways of using what they know about numbers, shapes, and so on, rather than insisting that results are reached by one fixed, ideal method.'

The passage could have been written by Dewey himself. Every element of his teaching is there: resistance to discrete subjects, the challenging of accepted authority, discovery by individual exploration.

The prestigious London Mathematical Society, in a report entitled 'Tackling the Mathematics Problem' published in October 1995, speaks of 'an unprecedented level of concern'. Yet the report remains shifty on causes. Though stating that Britain faces 'extremely serious problems' about the supply and preparation of entrants to university courses in mathematics, science, engineering and technology, it is careful to avoid any criticism of teachers. Indeed it insists at the outset that 'the main responsibility for the weaknesses we identify cannot be laid at the door of classroom teachers'. Such studious disclaimers, with their implication that no one in the educational system is to blame, are a polite convention typical of such studies. Yet the contents of the report contradict the disclaimers.

Condemning the proliferation of 'time-wasting activities

(investigations, problem-solving, data surveys, etc.) at the expense of core teaching', the report arrives at a startling conclusion, which can only be interpreted as a fundamental indictment of teaching methods and the philosophies that inform them:

> Most students entering higher education no longer understand that mathematics is a precise discipline in which exact, reliable calculation, logical exposition and proof play essential roles; yet it is these features that make mathematics important . . . One lecturer in engineering observed: 'Students have always made mistakes. The difference is that now, when I try to correct them, they do not believe me and there seems no way of convincing them. Some even insist that I must be wrong and they are right.'

Reluctance to recognise that the teacher may have superior qualifications to the student ('. . . For certain moral and intellectual purposes, adults must become like little children,' said Dewey), and the perpetual questioning of authority ('Traditionally mathematics have been about knowing the rules . . .' say the SEAC advisers) have helped to bring about a situation where students no longer understand that mathematics is a precise discipline, and in some cases to question *the very nature of proof itself.* Encouraging a questioning disposition from an early age is one thing: inculcating a form of irrationalism, something different. (The engineer's tale recalls Dostoyevsky's anarchic hero who questions whether two and two make four. What if they made five? Would it not be delightful, to escape from a mechanistic world? Put yourself what you believe to be five feet from a railway line when a train is passing, is the answer, and you will discover it.)

Complaints that large classes make the teacher's work more difficult may be justified. Yet as the *Guardian* editorial pointed out, one of the problems inherent in informal teaching methods is that they are labour-intensive. No increase in the number of teachers or reduction of pupils will overcome a conceptual disorder. If the 'laboratory' approach to education is misconceived for many purposes in the first place, then it will fail many children, no matter how much is invested in setting up or staffing the laboratory. If the relationship between teacher and pupil is that between Sun God and 'facilitator', even a one to one ratio might not be enough: Gods can be wilful and capricious, especially if young and over-indulged.

The truth is that Deweyism has been a gigantic experiment itself; the laboratory where it has been carried out, English state primary education. The experiment has been running for a third of a century. During roughly the same period hip-joint operations have become standard. Imagine what would have happened if a large percentage had 'come loose'. The loose of limb, acting together, would have forced the medical profession to review the entire procedure from top to bottom. In education no such logicality applies, and critics are nervous about linking causes and effects, presumably out of misplaced loyalty to their peers. The London Mathematical Society is aghast at the number of loose limbs, but squeamish about questioning the techniques used in the operation.

Had the millions on whom progressive theories have been tested to destruction included 'top people's' children, a halt would have been called long ago. For Conservatives it would be convenient to place the entire blame for what has happened on educational leftists and socialist governments, but the truth is more complex, and more revealing. Dewyism was imported wholesale into English primary practice as a result of the Plowden Report, and Lady Plowden, it is often forgotten, was appointed by a Conservative Government. If the teaching practices of prep schools had been the subject of her inquiry the Conservative Party would have done more than raise an eyebrow at her appointment; it would have moved to bar it. Someone of greater intellectual distinction, more able and ready to resist the pressures from the educational and social theorists of the day, would have been hastily located.

The story of the way the report was commissioned and Lady Plowden invested as chairwoman provides a remarkable insight into the casual, clubby way the educational destiny of the children of others can be decided. According to the *Sunday Times* (26 January 1992) the idea allegedly originated in an informal dinner between Sir Edward Boyle, then Minister for Education and a liberal patrician, and Lady Plowden. She is said to have told Sir Edward that she wished something could be done about 'our primary schools'. Sir Edward apparently responded by undertaking to set up an inquiry into primary education in all its aspects, including the transition to secondary schools. Legend has it that it was agreed, there and then, that Lady Plowden should be chairwoman.

About thirty academics and educational theorists with fashionable views were recruited, the accent being heavily weighted towards the 'new thinking' current in the sixties. When it reported to the Wilson Government in 1967, the ground was fertile for the acceptance of its recommendations: the move to comprehensives had already been decided, and the primary schools had to be dovetailed, albeit retrospectively, into the same philosophy.

If the *Sunday Times* is right, a report that was to set the tone for the early education of millions of children was conceived over dinner between a Conservative patrician and a member of the 'great and the good', and its implementation overseen by a socialist Minister. None of the three had any personal experience of state education. Their social consciences, it can reasonably be assumed, were inflected accordingly.

Had someone other than Lady Plowden been appointed, and a less partial group of advisers, it seems likely that reforms would still have been recommended and implemented. There might well have been an updating of teaching styles but it would have been tempered by caution: the stale bathwater would have been flushed away but not the infant with it. In any truly national education culture the great experiment with Deweyism in our primary schools would never have taken place. But then we do not have such a culture, and experiments in education are for carrying out on other people's children.

Not long ago I sat in at a history lesson in a primary school. The scene was familiar: brightly decorated classroom, ten-year-old pupils lounging round tables, their faces more indolent than sun-like, an air of amiable insouciance. The only surprising thing was that this was a rare example of 'whole-class' teaching. The lesson was on the French Resistance – an arbitrary and, it seemed to me, strangely ambitious project for ten-year-olds. No preparation had been done. It soon became clear that it wasn't needed.

The lesson consisted of the teacher asking the children how they would feel if their father had belonged to the Resistance. You could see in their eyes that the children had not given great thought to the matter.

'How would you feel if your father was called away on a mission against the Germans?'

Silence.

'You, Damien.'

Damien, roused from torpor, smirks.

'I wouldn't like it, miss.'

Damien nestles further back in his seat, his work done, his mental effort over. But the teacher presses him.

'*Why* wouldn't you like it?'

Damien knits his brow, slowly.

' 'Cos he might get killed.'

The teacher nods encouragingly. This was the sort of answer her question was designed to elicit. Her lesson was going well. She turns to a girl.

'And you? What would you think if your father went off one night with the French Resistance?'

'I wouldn't like it.'

'Why not?'

Silence. Then: ' 'Cos my mum and me would be alone.'

I reproduce this little scene as I recall it because it seems to me to encapsulate many of the problems of our primary education. It took place in the opposite of a deprived area: a country school where the children were overwhelmingly from middle-class families. The teacher, as far as I could see, was no left-wing zealot; she was merely implementing the national history curriculum. Her technique smacked of the 'empathy' method, by which children are supposed to gain historical awareness by placing themselves in the position of their subjects of study.

The teacher was obviously well intentioned, and the answers she wanted from the children were 'caring' ones. It was clear from the knowing look that children are too ingenuous to disguise that they were well aware of this and ready to oblige: 'He might get killed.' There was no evidence from their answers that they knew anything about the Second World War, apart perhaps from what they had seen on TV, or about France. Knowing was not the point of the lesson. They were expected simply to emote, and they did: 'My mum and me would be alone'.

The form of the lesson was no chance event. Titanic battles had been fought between 'progressives' and 'traditionalists' in the drawing up of this aspect of the primary curriculum. This was the result. Empathy was in, in spirit at least (it is not specifically mentioned in the National Curriculum) but out of respect for their professionalism teachers were allowed to implement the curriculum's requirements creatively. The way the teacher was approaching the French Resistance with her pupils was not dictated from above, by arbitrary authority, but her own creation. Other teachers might have thought of something more demanding. This one had not.

Like so many of the passionate arguments about the techniques of education, in the end the debate about 'empathy' is a non-discussion. The choice is not between having it and not having it. There can be no objection to the principle of putting yourself in the position of other people, living or dead, the better to understand their actions and motives. It is a routine technique, employed by storytellers, Method actors, even politicians. Sensibly used in schools it involves the imagination as well as the memory, engaging the children in what might otherwise be an arid and unappealing exercise in learning. What matters is the part it plays in the overall curriculum, the way it is done, and the level of achievement demanded.

As it happens I had seen the equivalent lesson in a French school, with pupils of a similar background and age (in fact they were a year junior). The subject was the French Revolution. The children were sitting in rows. They had well-produced books, with attractive pictures but also brief and intelligently chosen extracts from contemporary historical documents of the simpler and more personal kind. These they were required to read aloud, and discuss. One, I recall, was the text of a letter from a young aristocrat from her prison. It was well written, and included a sprinkling of words the children were not familiar with, which they had therefore to learn at home for the next lesson.

Their interest was not in doubt. Their emotions were caught by the image of a child languishing in prison, their intellect and imagination simultaneously engaged. Nor did the exercise preclude the learning by heart of the relevant dates. The chidren were sitting in rows as a means of ensuring attention, but there was no hint of pressurising about it – except to the extent that they were expected to concentrate and were not allowed to chat.

The teacher was no gorgon, and seemed as pleasant as her English counterpart. There was no sign that she was intent on translating theory into practice. She was just doing what seemed appropriate, choosing what she thought suitable for her class from a (no doubt centrally approved) book. After the brief lesson – it is no mystery of education that there is a limit on how far children can concentrate – they broke up for a less formal session, and left their rows. Later they would return.

The contrast in approach was total. The British children appeared bored by the lesson and learned virtually nothing, beyond how to regurgitate smarmily moralistic emotions on demand. The French seemed to enjoy the lesson, learned quite a bit, and memorised it to boot.

If I had asked the English teacher to explain her technique to me she would no doubt have done so eagerly, reproducing what she had learned on her course with that little air of imparting professional knowledge that the outside world would find paradoxical: that children can learn in informal surroundings, by casual discussion, without effort. And if I had questioned the procedure of asking for responses on a subject before that subject had been taught and learned, she might well have replied in the words of another teacher to whom I had put the same question.

Looking back at me, Dewey-eyed, the woman had replied: 'I don't teach subjects, I teach children.'

Had I given the history teacher the benefit of my amateur and inexpert opinion – that what she was doing was not just feeble in the extreme, but a tragic waste of time for herself and her pupils, who were capable of far greater effort – she would have marked me down as an educational Visigoth. Had I gone further and told her that she was in danger of inculcating a form of happy ignorance and anti-intellectualism from the earliest age, and that pupils with the good fortune to be taught in the private sector would be at a lifelong advantage, she would have been distressed and indignant. I would have been challenging her 'professionalism'. Above all she would have thought that, by suggesting a more systematic and demanding approach to learning, I was being 'unfeeling'.

I gave proof of my 'feelingness' by saying nothing. Where does one begin? And after all, I had not been invited to the school to inspect the lessons, but to examine a hole in the roof.

It is hard to argue with sentimentality. The very classrooms in our primaries are conceived as cocoons of innocence, where childishness is not something to grow out of, even as it is enjoyed, but to be perpetuated. Child-worship is a powerful strand in English culture (Wordsworth in poetry, Peter Pan), and the fact that an increasingly large number of teachers and educationalists have spent their entire lives in classrooms or institutes does little to promote maturation, either in themselves or their pupils.

The 'feelie' approach to education, however unworkably complex in the classroom, rests on simple assumptions. The good is in the child. Education is about bringing it out. An unduly rational approach would be emotional infanticide: as Wordsworth wrote, 'we murder to dissect'. The doctrine remains as romantically appealing today as in Rousseau's time. Suitably 'scientised', it becomes hard to contest without sounding both inexpert and hard of heart.

The assumption amongst teachers that outsiders intrude into

classroom theory with a mixture of brute ignorance and malicious intent is difficult to dispel. There is much touchiness and defensiveness about teaching styles. The slightest breath of criticism and it is at once concluded that the critics are intent on imposing Japanese methods of formality and mental coercion.

Yet the idea that a measure of gentleness and informality is desirable in dealing with young children is hardly a novel insight, confined to experts on education. We are not grappling with astrophysics but dealing with the sensible management and instruction of children, a subject in which millions have some practical experience. Today, for reasons Dewey did not foresee and which (it can be argued) are not disconnected from his emotionally indulgent approach, sensitive handling of children can be more necessary than ever. A glance at statistics of children living in broken homes shows that, even in primary schools in well-to-do areas, as many as 30 per cent of a class may be without one parent or another in their formative years.

At this point it becomes easy to become a little sentimental about teachers. More than ever before they can find themselves literally *in loco parentis*. Outside pressures of every kind mean that the child entering primary school for the first time today is likely to be a world away from the fresh, sunny mind presupposed in Dewey's writings.

TV violence, commercialised sex, bad diets, and the frequent absence of nursery education – all these things combine to make the primary school teacher's job harder. As one teacher of children from a difficult housing estate told me ruefully, while politicians were busy discussing how to inculcate the 'basics' of numeracy and literacy, she was busy with something more basic still: teaching five-year-olds how to tie their shoelaces, and above all encouraging them to *talk*. Many were not in the habit of being spoken to, having spent much of their first five years alone in front of the TV.

It is impossible not to sympathise. Yet a realistic understanding of what teachers can face in their everyday work is no excuse for a pitying over-indulgence towards the profession. If life is frequently hard for them, and not only in inner cities, all the more reason not to impose on them the additional burden of unworkable methods.

Not all our primary schools, of course, are alike, and some have managed to retain more traditional and more effective teaching styles, without being in any sense reactionary. Yet the supply of older teachers who have undergone and been trained in this type of schooling themselves is coming to an end. As the generations change the "new" fashion is in danger of becoming a near-monopoly. Hence the current crisis.

Would a General Teachers' Council, often proposed by teachers to boost their status, improve things? Not while the present uncertainties hang over the professionalism of the profession. The problem is not one of image but of substance. For example a familiar response to informed public criticism of teaching philosophies is that, in adopting this style or that, teachers are merely selecting from a range of methods they have learned. That may well be the case, and teachers may not be individually to blame. Yet the defence is inadequate.

Again, a medical analogy suggests itself. If a surgeon took off a leg without anaesthetic we would see it as no defence to say that he was simply using one of many options at his disposal: we would be astonished that such an option should be considered appropriate in any circumstances, and begin asking questions about the state of the entire profession. And if we suspected that his action – and the General Medical Council's stalwart defence of it on the grounds that some surgeons took off legs one way, others another – was in fact dictated by adherence to a theory of medicine widely seen as quackery, the shift to private medicine would be sudden and vast.

In a sense, that is what is happening in education. Before it can rely on public respect or seek to encourage that respect through the establishment of a General Teachers' Council, the educational profession must heal itself.

The most depressing statistic I have heard about state primary education has nothing to do with the results of national tests in maths or reading. It was in the 'creative' realm in which our state primaries are meant to excel. A few years ago an art competition was held between children at primary schools, state and private. The great day came, and to general embarrassment, all the prizes went to children at private schools.

The judges, needless to say, had no knowledge of their backgrounds, nor were they the kind of people to be taken in by bland, over-tutored work. It is impossible to believe that the distribution of artistic talent is so concentrated amongst privileged children in fee-paying schools, or that ethnic problems or 'better facilities' are the explanation. Even in art (one might say especially in art) informality and good intentions are not enough. You have to work at it.

The truth is that some state primaries have ceased being schools by any reasonable definition. The impression one gains, now borne out by official tests, is that they are merely playing at schools. The English, it is said, make bad ideologues. It is a failing in which we should take a stubborn pride. We certainly do not seem to be very good at educational theories. Maybe we should give them up, revert to our true nature and do what seems sensible?

CHAPTER EIGHT

The Comprehensive Folly

> 'The characteristic of the hour is that the commonplace mind, knowing itself to be commonplace, has the assurance to proclaim the rights of the commonplace and to impose them wherever it will.'
>
> *(Ortega Y Gasset, The Revolt of the Masses)*

* * *

As Minister for Higher Education I was once despatched by Margaret Thatcher to China, where I had worked as a diplomat during the Cultural Revolution. The purpose was to represent her at the opening ceremony of a new university at Ningpo, a former British possession to the south of Shanghai and birthplace of her friend, the recently deceased Hong Kong billionaire and philanthopist Y. K. Pao. He had donated the entire university to his home town in the way that others would donate a library or lecture room.

I took the opportunity of a seat on Y. K. Pao's private plane to go on to Peking to discuss education policy with the Chinese Minister. He was trying to repair the ravages of the Cultural Revolution and was interested in British experience. Though obviously well briefed on our secondary schools, he was a puzzled man. Before I could question him about what was going on in Chinese education he said: 'There is something you must explain to me. I am told that you send all secondary children to the same type of school. Is this correct?'

He glanced tetchily at his advisers, as if doubting the accuracy of his brief and hoping I would show they had got it wrong. I replied that, broadly speaking, it was correct. The schools were called comprehensives.

'So children with completely different abilities go to the same schools?'

That indeed, I said, was the case. There followed a silence. It is a fallacy that the Chinese try and succeed in hiding their emotions on all occasions. The Minister's face was a caricature of incredulity.

'I am further told that you put children of different abilities not just in the same schools, but . . .' he glanced at his advisers again, as if afraid they had made him look silly . . . '*In the same classes.*'

That too, I replied, was often done.

'Oh.'

The Minister declined to take things further: causing foreign guests embarrassment by pressing them on their curious customs would be impolite. Already I felt like Marco Polo describing inexplicable Western practices to Kublai Khan.

It is not difficult to understand the Minister's amazement. As in our primary schools, so in our secondary education we take things to extremes. Comprehensive schools, English style, reveal us as more dogmatic than the communists, more moralistic than the Americans and more insistent on the precedence of theory over practice than the French. In education we jettison not just our sceptical traditions but our natural *sang froid*, becoming strangely emotional. Defenders of comprehensive schools are not simply in favour of them: they are invariably *committed* to them. Indeed they are *passionately* committed to them, and their commitment is not just to one system of education over another, it is to the comprehensive *ideal*. And from ideals, as we know, no deviation is tolerable.

The English are less passionate than they should be about education but are unsurpassed in their strength of feeling about the structure of their schools. Here they are brimful of fervour, be it in defence of parents to send their children to independent institutions or of 'the comprehensive ideal'. The emotionalism is not confined to untrained or uncritical minds. Anthony Crosland, the intelligent, well-born and privately educated Labour Minister for Education, famously told his wife: 'If it's the last thing I do, I am going to destroy every fucking grammar school in England. And Wales. And Northern Ireland.'

'Destroy?' 'Fucking?' Whence this virulence about schools that, whatever you think of them sociologically, were good at education, producing some of the most impressive people on the front bench of today's Labour Party? Do these proto-Ministers feel as guilty about their educational provenance as Crosland seems to have felt about his? Do Tony Blair and Harriet Harman feel guilty too about sending their children to the wrong kind of school? Will their children be made to feel guilty in turn? In education as in sex our capacity for guilt, and for the contorted thinking it induces, seems never-ending. If we are ever to make a success of our secondary schools, leaving guilt and emotion behind is an essential preliminary. The only people whose conscience should trouble them are those who evade the truth about what makes one school bad and another good, while sending their children to the good ones and leaving the bad to the rest.

The reason Anthony Crosland expressed himself as he did had of course little to do with education and everything to do with class. 'Every fucking grammar school in England . . .' The demotic idiom says it all. Old attitudes die hard in education and thirty years later the strong feeling continues to show through the blandest commentary on comprehensives. In his briefing paper on selection submitted to the National Commission On Education in 1992, Dr Geoffrey Walford of Aston University, after arguing – rather effectively it seems to me – against a haphazard return to selection that could result from current Government policy, concludes a rational discussion with what seems little more than an expression of faith: 'The claim that comprehensives have led to a decline in overall educational standards is not proved. The most reasonable conclusion is that the more truly comprehensive the system, the more likely it is to have led to a small overall improvement.'

The modesty of the claim – 'a small overall improvement' – is unsettling. Something better than that might have been expected after thirty years. In the light of these slow and uncertain benefits the call to take the revolution further in the search for a 'more truly comprehensive' system borders on the irrational: you do not plunge ahead with a philosophy of schooling that has delivered no more than a small improvement in thirty years.

What if the judgment erred on the side of optimism? – and given the author's evident commitment to the comprehensive ideal an element of wishful thinking cannot be excluded. What if it turned out that what he took for a borderline improvement proved to have been an overall deterioration? Assessment of a system of education in which many experts believe for what are primarily non-educational reasons (Dr Walford speaks at one point of the 'social and academic effectiveness' of schools – note the order) are notoriously subjective. Are we to march ahead resolutely on the egalitarian road on the basis of such flimsy and (possibly) partial evidence?

Again it is important not to underestimate the personal factor. For believers in the comprehensive doctrine it becomes impossible to accept that the 'ideal' has failed in over a third of a century of practice. Personal as much as intellectual reasons can make it hard for such people to recognise that the very system that was designed to help the weak and underprivileged, and to which they may have devoted much of their lives, has had the reverse effect. The same was true of many communists. I do not confuse defenders of comprehensives with communists, yet it is a striking fact that when contemplating the failure of their ideas both tend to give the same answer: 'It was never tried'.

The tower blocks of the sixties were not built as homes for people to live in. They were designed to provide units of accommodation – a very different thing – and to enable governments of the Left and Right to out-build each other quickly and cheaply, the better to impress the electorate. Today we wonder how we could ever have been so lacking in imagination as to suppose that what looked alluring as an architect's model, with its toy trees and plastic grass, could be transposed into life: how inherently inhuman structures could create a human community. Watching the high-rises being dynamited we experience a triple pleasure. Together with revulsion at their hideousness and interest in how the monsters will fall, we feel a frisson of righteousness. Humanity has won over the outsize, the ugly and the abstract.

Comprehensives are the equivalent of the high-rise blocks in education. On the drawing board of our educational architects they looked enticingly modern. Realised in practice, the worst amongst them resemble the high-rises tipped on to on their sides – building blocks set down and assembled with a purposeful social hand. There is a strange disproportion between the living and educational quarters: the high-rises seem too high and the comprehensives too squat, as if their earth-hugging quality were designed to emphasize their levelling aspirations. The featurelessness of their facades announces a gaunt, egalitarian purpose, and just as the tower-blocks incarcerated their inhabitants in 'living units', so many such schools turned into centres of social detention: for many able pupils education was no longer a way out.

The flats were an experiment in living in the same way that the secondary schools, like the primaries, were educational laboratories. The crucial thing they had in common was that in no circumstances could the people who conceived and built them imagine themselves living in the tower blocks or sending their children to the schools. Not all schools conformed to this abstract model, and there were (and are) many kinds of comprehensive. Some of them are former grammar schools, and in better-off areas ingenious ways were found to vary the contents while retaining the pietistic label; another example of how social hypocrisy infects our education. (A parallel suggests itself in our quaint tradition of describing our most exclusive private schools as 'public'.)

The London Oratory, of recent notoriety as the choice of the Blairs for their son, is an egregious example. It still regards itself as a comprehensive, though it is notably short of the essential characteristics. In 1947, when they were already a matter of debate, comprehensives were defined as local schools intended to cater for all children in a given area, much as a milkman or postman would service a set number of streets. In few senses is the London Oratory a local school. Nor is it for all children: its Catholic denomination and heavy parental demand ensure that it has greater control of entry. Rebuked for failing to describe it in the terms in which the school saw itself, the *Daily Express* was contrite, agreeing that the London Oratory was indeed a comprehensive, in the same sense that the Queen was an old age pensioner living in Westminster.

Predictably it was those at the bottom, in socially homogenous areas, who bore the brunt of the experiment. Equally predictably at that level at least comprehensive schools have been counterproductive. Instead of liberating people from educational and social deprivation, in the worst areas they ghettoised them. Instead of spreading equality they emphasised and perpetuated the difference between 'us' and 'them'. Instead of providing attractive communities they were places you fled from if you possibly could. So it is that the worst of our comprehensives have come to symbolise the social divisions they were designed to overcome. It is a common observation that if people are perpetually surrounded by ugliness they stop seeing it, and cease to understand the depressive effect ugliness has on them. What is true of uninspired buildings is true of unaspiring education. People become accustomed, and the cycle of deprivation continues.

The impact of a uniform, centrally imposed philosophy of instruction goes wider. You cannot squeeze whole segments of society through a standardised mill without the consequences showing, and the results of thirty years of socially rather than technically or academically based schooling can be seen in the exultation of ordinariness that characterises much of British culture. Stereotyped clothes and accents, the ingratiating sportiness of politicians, the soothing introductions to classical music on the radio ('This is not going to hurt, you might even grow to like it'), and the steady gravitation of the quality press towards middlebrow values make it ironic to hear both John Major and Tony Blair pledge themselves to work tirelessly in the cause of a classless society. Culturally and intellectually, we already have it. The matrix of massification is set in place from our earliest years.

To some these sentiments will sound elitist. It depends what you mean. An 'elite' is defined in the Oxford English Dictionary as the 'choice part of society', which has connotations of exclusivity. What I am saying is the opposite: namely that individuals, wherever they stand on the social scale, should enjoy an equal right to have their talents developed through diverse, demanding, high-quality education, and were that to happen their lives, tastes and personal cultures would be more variegated and less open to commercial and political manipulation than they currently are.

Thc manipulation, it goes without saying, is frequently accomplished by those who see themselves as the choice part of society. For example a recent editorial in *The Times* (28 May 1996) defended the fanning of nationalist sentiment over Europe by Conservative politicians on the grounds that Disraeli and Salisbury had never hesitated to appeal to what the newspaper called the *vulgus* in prosecuting their foreign policies. The writer, in his or her patriotic exultation, appears momentarily to have forgotten that we live at the end of the twentieth century, when Britain is supposed to be an educated democracy.

The fact that what should be the merest platitudes about the need to equip individuals through their schooling to transcend the drab norm cannot be spoken in Britain without sounding elitist is a measure of how our climate of conformity has solidified into a mental code. It is important to remember how far we have strayed from common sense, and from common practice in other countries. The negative associations that will be triggered by such phrases as 'personal culture' would be mystifying to much of the rest of the world – with the exception, of course, of our egalitarian co-religionaries in the United States of America, whose schools are not regarded by anyone as a model.

There are strong grounds for suspecting that neither Major nor Blair (despite the latter's protestations) believes in comprehensive schooling as it is commonly practised, or indeed at all. It is a strange country where the leaders of the main political parties nurse doubts about the dominant system of secondary education, while feeling compelled to avoid saying so openly. The explanation for their reticence is clearly to some extent party political – Blair's problems with his backbenchers, and Major's reluctance to rile the teacher unions more than is inevitable. But there is more to it than that.

This is one of those occasions when politicians of the Left and Right suspect that something in our society is profoundly wrong, but are fearful of going against the grain of accepted opinion by revealing their views. The problem with stating the truth about comprehensives is that there is little evidence that the public are seriously dissatisfied with them. Polls show exactly what you would expect: that there is a majority for selective education in theory but a minority in practice. 'Bring back the grammar schools' evokes easy applause, but when the opportunity arises to change the status of a local comprehensive, most frequently the voting is against. Not long ago this happened in Major's own constituency.

To say that people have grown to love their comprehensives as much as they love their NHS or their mortgage tax relief would be an exaggeration. A more plausible explanation is that cultures become embedded, almost irrespective of their worth. That is what happened in our cosy but educationally disastrous primary schools. People become attuned to the familiar, and feel secure with it. For the majority of mortals security is preferable to risk and responsibility, and for the English, with their over-developed social conscience and under-developed aspirations in education, the risk of 'unfairness' and 'divisiveness' in the way we allocate children to schools takes precedence over any possible gain from change. The ultimate security is to be like everyone else, and that is what the present system offers. Whether standardised schooling is good for us, individually or nationally, or in the long term viable as the world presses on our heels, is another matter.

When people say that 'the comprehensive did all right by my child' they may well be correct: what they most frequently mean is that it provided a middling education for what may have been a middle-ability pupil. This too may well have been the case. The problem is where that middle lies. International comparisons suggest that in Britain it lies pretty low, in vocational education, as well as in the humanities.

National evaluations are beginning to tell us something similar, and not just about performance at the bottom of the pile in deprived areas: 'Many parents, often in leafy middle-class suburbs, accept standards which are too low.' So wrote Christopher Woodhead, HM Chief Inspector of Schools, in his pamphlet *A Question of Standards, Finding the Balance* (Politeia, 1995). The latest Ofsted report on secondary education includes the bald statement: 'Standards taken across all subjects require improvement in about two-fifths of secondary schools.'

Since there are 3,500 such schools in all, this means that 1,400 schools are teaching a million or more pupils to sub-standard levels. Far from contradicting him (and it is revealing that the Opposition front bench studiously refrain from attacks on the 'controversial' Christopher Woodhead), the Labour spokesman, David Blunkett, is beginning to speak the same language, excoriating low achievement, especially in comprehensives.

If a survey were to conclude that 40 per cent of private schools dispensed sub-standard education, the reaction would be immediate. ISIS would have a hard time resisting pressure to reveal the names of the schools in question, and justifying the fees demanded in return for faulty education. Alarmed at the thought of their children failing to get a place in higher education, parents might propose paying 60 per cent of their fees till the question of standards was cleared up, and dramatic improvements made. In the state sector expectations are different.

In a type of schooling where competition is disliked and distrusted, peaks and troughs become more difficult to recognise, whether by parents or anyone else. The whole point of the system is to smooth out the peaks and the troughs. In this way the average becomes the summit of achievement. For many years this philosophy was reflected in the vocabulary of the Inspectors. In the seventies and eighties HMI was part of the drive against making comprehensives 'grammar schools for all', and Heads got bad reports for using methods that were considered 'too didactic'. Since the dictionary definition of 'didactic' is 'having the character or manner of a teacher; characterised by giving instruction' we had wandered a long way from the essence of things. 'Good practice' came to mean the avoidance of academic methods, and the work of schools who conformed was consistently described as being 'satisfactory or better'.

Satisfactory in relation to what? We have learned to be sceptical. It is no use leaving the judgment to parents. In a sense they can be the last people to decide what may or may not be 'satisfactory'; it was not through parental pressures that the shortcomings in primary education were identified. In a secondary system originally devised to minimise competition in and between schools, parents who are themselves increasingly the products of those schools are unlikely to be over-demanding. Low or middling aspirations can become self-generating as we move from one comprehensively educated generation to another. The idea that parents are vigilant about standards and active in their defence is a prime example of political voluntarism: it may need to be said for exhortatory reasons, but saying it does not make it true.

A simple example of how modest ambitions perpertuate themselves is in English literature. Here every teacher with a second or third-class degree – assuming they have one at all – is encouraged to believe that he or she is entitled to re-invent the canon. If as a result expectations in schools are middling to low the consequences will be cyclical, as middle-brow writing tends to become accepted as literature in the finest sense. The result will be a confusion of categories, as mediocrity becomes not simply the norm, but the height of achievement. In line with the nostrums of social relevance 'contemporary literary achievements' must naturally be reflected in the curriculum and in examination syllabuses. The pupil finds the writing 'accessible', produces the conventional responses, the circle moves on, and everyone is content. Objections will be dismissed as sniffy and undemocratic.

Anecdotal experience bears out these fears of passive acceptance of indifferent standards. Like all MPs I have frequently been lobbied by parents about their schools. Like many colleagues in less advantaged constituencies than my own, I receive complaints that are almost invariably about buildings, facilities, class sizes and the rest. Only rarely do people voice concern about levels of education, one reason being that those most likely to do so have made the appropriate decision. By and large the public take what they are given, and not always because they are verbally bamboozled by educators into accepting it. The truth is that there is a limit as to how far they are concerned: not the least of the disadvantages of egalitarianism in education is that what was good enough for oneself can come to be seen as good enough for one's children.

Once I was summoned by parents and teachers to a meeting to discuss the school's playground. The problem was that it sloped. Children, I was told indignantly by one of the twenty or thirty parents who turned out, could fall and hurt themselves. I pointed out that the playground was grassed, and asked if any child had come to grief. None had. I said I would see what could be done, while indicating that I had seen schools with bigger problems.

I then asked the parents if they were happy with the school. How, for example, were grammar and technology taught? (The school, I had heard, was undistinguished in these areas.) The answer was a general mystification in my decidedly middle-class audience as to the meaning of the question. Low expectations are no monopoly of the 'lower classes'. Had the children of fee-paying parents attended the school there might well have been expressions of dissatisfaction from articulate and demanding (i.e. 'pushy') parents, from which the children of all might have ultimately benefited. As it was there was puzzled silence.

Was this an overhang from the years when parents had few means to judge the performance of a school other than by its physical appearance, and when the tendency was to equate good schools with good facilities? It must be hoped that the publication of examination results, crude as the measure is, will help to erode such complacent attitudes.

If John Major and Tony Blair were to find themselves members of my imaginary Committee for the Improvement of State Education, and could do what they liked free of party and public pressures, there seems little doubt that they would come to similar conclusions. On secondary schools they would agree without difficulty that:

(1) The comprehensive model, as implemented in Britain, has been a failure overall.
(2) The system replacing it must put educational rather than social aspirations to the fore, since improvements in the latter field depend on the former.
(3) While there can be no going back to the grammar school/ secondary modern school model, some form of selection must nevertheless be reintroduced.

There are words, so barnacled with controversy that to speak them is like clasping a seashell to your ear: instantly you hear echoes of angry tides and roaring battles. 'Selection' is one such word. In Britain the echoes are always the same, the associations automatic. Selection has become a *down* word, more often evoking failure than success. It conjures up not the excellence of those who are chosen but the affront to those who are not. Mention the word in an educational context and in conventionally-minded company and the rest of the discussion is preordained: 'unfair', 'rejects consigned to the scrap heap', 'badge of failure . . .'

The reflex is rational to the extent that our experience of the eleven-plus examination was positive for the minority and negative for the rest. To the extent that no political party aspires to return to that system, or anything like it, the reaction is illogical, suggesting that once again we are intent on reliving the past rather than confronting the future.

In economics a parallel taboo exists on the more minor matter of VAT on children's shoes. The image of barefoot children at the beginning of the century interdicts rational debate. It is no use pointing out that taxing children's shoes and devoting the proceeds (minus compensation for those on income support) to education would make excellent sense, or that parents in other countries pay a sales tax on their children's footwear along with everything else. Guilty memories are the hardest to erase; in a sense we treasure them, as proof of our virtue. We may be insufficiently ambitious about our children's education, but never shall we sink to the point of putting VAT on their shoes!

To say that there has always been and will always be selection in choral schools, sport or the Booker prize is to state a tiresome but necessary truth. In education the point should not be to devise ever more subtle means of escaping the inevitable but to find ways of applying selection, sensitively and equitably, to our schools, just as we have done, with great success, in our universities.

At the start of this section I imagined what might happen if users of private schools were to reconstruct the education system from scratch. The closest we have come to the experiment of 'beginning again from the beginning' in a way which involves the higher echelons of society was when Robert Birley (1903–1982) was Educational Adviser to the British Military Government in post-war Germany. Subsequently he became Head of Eton.

Known for his mildly dissenting views as 'Red Birley', he was given an opportunity to influence the reconstruction of an education system in a country parts of which had almost literally been reduced to a *tabula rasa*. The contrast between what was done there and what was simultaneously happening in Britain in the wake of the 1944 Education Act provides crucial clues about the source of our post-war failures, and is therefore still relevant today. In deciding where to go it is important to remind ourselves where we have come from.

In Germany, the result of our efforts, co-ordinated with those of the French and the Americans (there was some falling out with the Russians) was the creation in what was to become West Germany of a central system of education administered by the *Länder*, with local variations. In general there are three types of school: the *Hauptschule*, akin to our secondary modern; the *Realschule*, more technical and more aspiring; and the

Gymnasium, a grammar-type school. There has of course been evolution, with a minority of *Länder* having a comprehensive system, while others have abolished the *Hauptschule* as being insufficiently demanding, leaving two types of school.

For the British, with their social sensitivities, the fly in the ointment would be the selective nature of the system. But 'selection' in Germany carries few of the negative overtones it has in Britain, and is a far more sophisticated affair than our eleven-plus examination. The mode of selection is less arbitrary in its methods and final in its implications.

The decision is made over two or more years, depending on the *Land* in question, during what are called orientation stages from the age of ten to twelve. It is not based on simple examination but on the child's general level of attainment and the recommendation of teachers in consultation with parents; indeed the parents often have the final choice, on the understanding that there is little point in opting for too academic an education if the child cannot keep up, or insisting that he or she wants to be an engineer or a doctor if they have no practical bent.

Selective education as we understand it often comes into practice only at the age of fourteen. After the two-year 'orientation' stage the pupils at the various types of school follow a broadly similar curriculum. This enables any necessary reassessment to take place, and the transfer of a child to a different school, given the inconvenient fact that different children develop at different rates. This is a long way from the 'once and for all decision, taken on the basis of a single examination but affecting the rest of a child's life' of eleven-plus notoriety.

The German model, though like all models imperfect, seems as close as one can get to a fail-safe system of selection. It is made less on grounds of raw ability than of aptitude demonstrated in practice, though naturally the two can blur. Not to get into a *Gymnasium* (grammar school) does not mean – as it effectively meant in Britain – banishment to educational darkness. A *Realschule* (technical) education may result in a career as a scientist or electronic engineer.

The main lesson for us concerns the prestige attached to technical education. One of the inherited characteristics that conditioned the reconstruction of education in post-war Germany was the pre-war success of the vocational schools which had helped make the country such a formidable enemy. That the British were very alive to the importance of technical education, in Germany at least, is evident from records of the period. In the words of a Senior Education Control Officer in Germany, J. A Sutherland, written in 1947: 'Although we live in a technical age whose problems are closely related to the spectacular advances in technology in recent years, the importance of Technical and Vocational Education is not generally realised, even amongst those most closely concerned with education today.'

While the Germans, with British guidance and acquiescence, set up in the post-war years a system of education that has served them well, at home the British stumbled from one failure to another. The 1944 Education Act was a botched and in practice largely abortive attempt to set up the kind of tripartite arrangement that was to prove so successful in Germany. In reality everything was left to the diligence of underfunded and often lackadaisical local authorities. The crucial element of the tripartite system – the technical schools – was our biggest failure. While the grammar schools increased their places faster than the school population, two decades after the war a mere 2 per cent of that population were receiving technical schooling. The year the last technical school closed, 1955, was a baleful year in English education.

The rest is familiar: the third leg, the secondary moderns, developed into what were widely seen as schools for academic rejects, with low budgets and big classes and where much carpentry was done. The great gulf in English education between a well-taught academic elite and the under-educated remainder, instead of being bridged in a way that suited the ability of pupils and prepared a war-weakened country for the economic challenges to come, was further entrenched. The consequences remain with us to this day. Intensive study by the National Institute of Economic and Social Research has shown alarming discrepancies between Britain and Germany, especially at craftsman and technician level, and in mathematics.

In 1964, the year before the introduction of comprehensives, a survey carried out by the International Association for the Evaluation of Educational Achievement (IEA) revealed that 24 per cent of English pupils fell into the category of low achievers, compared with 8–10 per cent in Germany, the Netherlands and Japan, and 14 per cent in France. Overall, English students were assessed as being two years behind their German equivalents, even though the Germans start primary school a year later, at six years old. In 1981, after sixteen years of comprehensives, in twenty-nine out of thirty-seven basic questions English pupils did significantly worse than in 1964.

More recent surveys suggest that the gap persists. The 1995 report by the London Mathematical Society quoted in Chapter 7 concluded a passage on international comparisons by stating:

> Many countries are concerned about recruitment to science and mathematic undergraduate courses. However, it would appear that the important aim of sending mathematically competent students to university to study quantitative subjects is being more satisfactorily met elsewhere than it is in the UK. It is essential that our national aims and objectives for education in mathematics should take full account of what is being achieved in other countries.

Viewed against German attainments, the Society's concerns are understandable. In the late eighties German universities produced 26,000 engineers and technology graduates; in Britain the figure was 16,000. In medicine, health and other vocational studies the figures were: Germany 21,400, Britain 13,500. The two areas where the British were ahead were languages and the arts (29,000 to the German 12,000) and science (27,000 to 13,000).

The picture is not black and white. The fact that we outproduce the Germans in scientists would seem cause for self-congratulation, even more so when one considers the reputation of those scientists at their best. Yet one part of education cannot be seen in isolation from another. Our failure to translate scientific excellence into economic prosperity is legendary. As we seek for reasons we should remember that from 1976 to 1988 two-thirds of the British workforce had no vocational qualifications at all, compared to a third in Germany. France, which for some years has had separate technical schools – *lycées professionnels* – has performed less well than the Germans but better than the British (the fact that the same was for a long time true of the French economy is suggestive). In the light of all this, producing three times as many graduates in education as Germany seems to have been a doubtful advantage.

Sutherland's simple truths about the new technical age were applied to our erstwhile adversary though not at home. Having improvised our way (with much help from across the Atlantic) into winning the war, we declined to draw conclusions about what constitutes a powerful modern nation, and immediately slipped back into our languorous ways. The consequences were to prove momentous. If effort and money and foresight had been invested in high-grade technical education in those decisive years the benefits would have been immense, both in our economy and throughout our educational culture.

It would have helped to erode the anti-industrial ethos, brilliantly described by Martin Wiener in his book *English Culture and the Decline of the Industrial Spirit* and in Corelli Barnet's *The Audit of War*. 'Parity of esteem between vocational and academic education', instead of being an empty cliché, already current in government studies in 1944, might have become a reality.

A better trained and qualified workforce would have made it less likely that we would find ourselves in the nineties without a single mass-market car manufacturer in British ownership, with no home-based British electronics industry that can begin to rival those of the Pacific Rim, despite our national flair for software, and with exports to emerging markets such as China below those of Germany, France and Italy. Many people would have been richer, and the poor less poor. Nor would we be reduced to making a virtue of necessity, as the Government does, by boasting that we are a low-cost, low-wage economy, when what we should surely be aiming at are high skills, high quality, and high rewards for entrepreneurs and workforce alike.

In Britain even the teaching of vocational studies, such as hairdressing and plumbing, or electronics, becomes a matter of doctrinal disputation. Though the Government has sought to give a higher status to the National Vocational Qualification (NVQ) and General National Vocational Qualification (GNVQ), it finds itself haunted, here too, by the ghost of Dewey. Formal teaching is resisted. There is no set content or fixed body of knowledge for many such studies, and often no written test. Examination more frequently takes the form of competence to do the job, to be assessed by teachers, and different teachers assess at different levels. The result, inevitably, is to compound the difficulty of encouraging pupils and employers to take the NVQ and GNVQ examinations seriously.

It is part of the crudity that characterises our education debate that technical instruction is automatically counterposed to education in the liberal arts, as if society had to choose. Since we have been under-performing in technology, the argument goes, we must put less stress on the humanities and arts and more on economically relevant subjects. The image of Britain as a country with its eyes fixed irremovably on the higher ideals of learning, a nation of *littérateurs* and high-domed philosophers disdainful of the material demands of modernity, is beguiling, but hard to situate. What we appear to forget is that it is possible to be neither one thing nor the other: a relatively low-tech country, with a low-brow culture.

Had we faced up to the necessity of advanced technical schools in those lost years, the humanities would have ultimately benefited too. High levels of academic education would not have come to be seen as 'privileged' or 'elitist' – a barbarous notion – in a system where equally-demanding opportunities would have been open to all in the fields where their talents lay. Politically, a more enlightened approach to different types of education would have had the immeasurable advantage of soothing the consciences of left-wing intellectuals. Egalitarian pressures would have been weaker as a result, so that Anthony Crosland would never have felt moved to utter his oath of destruction against grammar schools.

Comprehensives would never have been imposed across the entire system with such vengeful zeal if 'all-in education' had not become a matter of social and political doctrine; and if an academic education had remained an option for those whose aptitudes lay that way, the great divide in our education would have been much less wide and deep than it has subsequently become. The private sector (which Anthony Crosland left untouched), it might never have become the escape route for the professional and managerial classes in flight from the comprehensives, and independent schools might have found it less easy to establish their ascendancy in the absence of competition from the state.

The contrast between our post-war vision abroad and our short-sighted complacency at home grows more striking with the years. Few sins of omission have had such damaging consequences. How could an entire nation have been so blind to the seemingly obvious? It is not necessary to be a class warrior, or indeed a left-winger at all, to suspect that our great post-war failure in education may have had something to do with the fact that the power and moneyed elite in Britain had no direct personal stake in its state system at all – any more than it has today.

The one thing we cannot do is to go back and start again. To explain that comprehensives were all an unfortunate historical mistake would give rise to understandable confusion amongst teachers and parents. Even if there were a consensus for doing so there is no realistic option of transforming our secondary schools at a stroke into a tripartite, German-style system. We have to build on what we have got. This means working from the top and the bottom simultaneously to mould a divided system into a rich and diverse whole.

As we have seen, no political party has yet displayed the will or imagination to grasp the nettle of private education. In the state sector, however, there are signs of a more enlightened understanding of what is wrong, and of a creeping convergence of thinking between the parties. It is increasingly clear that Labour and Conservative front benches start from a similar assumption: the need to move towards a more diverse system. To the chagrin of his more traditionalist colleagues, Tony Blair has implicitly endorsed much that the Government have done to introduce choice and to give individual schools greater autonomy. This overlapping of analysis and prescription was reflected in Labour's hesitations and ambiguities over whether or not to abolish grant-maintained schools; more recently it was evident in Blair's criticisms of comprehensives, and in his interest in developing specialist schools.

Progress nevertheless remains tentative, and its limits easily defined. Party pressures continue to prevent Blair from opening up a more sophisticated discussion on selection, which diversification and greater emphasis on technical studies will necessarily involve. The imbroglio over his health spokeswoman, Harriet Harman, sending her child to a selective in preference to a comprehensive school reminded him, if he needed reminding, of what is currently possible.

It is hard to overstate the symbolism of that event. The Harman affair was Labour's Dreyfus Case, a controversy that transcended the individual and called attention to a deeper malaise. The media concentrated on the question of hypocrisy, yet the real lesson of the affair was the persistence of hidebound thinking in Labour on education. The furore surrounding the choice of a single MP to send her children to a particular state school, and the parliamentary recriminations and scenes of bitterness within Labour that it evoked, are a measure of our educational atavism. It could have happened in no country but our own. As was clear from the personalities involved, this was an instance of class conflict within the Left. In the light of the spectacle, those who believe that class is no longer an issue in late-twentieth-century Britain carry all the conviction of the Frenchmen who claimed at the time of the Dreyfus case that anti-Semitism was not rife in late-nineteenth-century France.

What the Left as a whole has still to understand is that the commitment to the 'comprehensive ideal' is old thinking in a Labour Party that is supposed to be new. A measure of its antiquity is that enthusiasm for the idea of a uniform system of education dates back to about the time when, in economic policy, the 'workers' self-management' movement in Yugoslavia was all the rage on the British and Continental left.

Antipathy to selection in any form will continue to block a solution to the state/private divide, should Labour come to power, as well as progress within the state sector itself. Yet nothing lasts for ever. One day Labour, in or out of office, will have to face up to realities. Dark memories of the eleven-plus will finally have to give way to a mature debate about the recruitment of children to more or less specialised schools, or to specialised sections within the same school, on a basis of aptitude, in the way the Conservatives are already discussing.

For Labour, finding suitable words to change the terms of the debate will be the key. It is possible to foresee ways in which congealed vocabularies will be subtly unfrozen. Already the Labour leadership is talking about 'diversity within one campus' (oblivious, it seems, to the echoes of Stalin's famous call for 'socialism in one country' – itself a measure of ideological retreat and retrenchment). One day, perhaps, the bogeyman phrase 'selection by ability' will be replaced by something more positive-sounding and electorally seductive: 'entry by aptitude', perhaps?

For Labour traditionalists to take a stand on principle, closing their eyes to foreign experience and insisting on Britain's educational specificity, would be as futile as it is for the Tories to blind themselves eternally to the debilitating effects of segregation. There is as much hope of maintaining Britain as an island of educational egalitarianism in a sea of selection as of reviving our empire in the East.

The comparison is not arbitrary. The pressures of competitive economies, many in Asia, will one day impose a solution to a question that decades of class wars in education have failed to resolve. When not only the Germans and Japanese but a billion Chinese (whose ancient meritocratic traditions have left them with few inhibitions about selection) are producing a greater number of better-trained motor mechanics or computer engineers than ourselves, and our import and employment figures reflect their superiority, it will not be enough for reactionaries of the Left or Right to strike heroic stances, and to cry 'over my dead body'.

Technological determinism is a powerful force: obliged to draw on all its reserves of skills and brains to stay in the race, one day even the British will end up seeking out and nurturing talent, whatever form that talent takes and at whatever level of society it is found, from an early age.

Escapism in the Conservative Party takes different forms. Though they have occupied the high intellectual ground on diversification and choice in the state sector, pulling Labour reluctantly up behind them, sectional interest prevents them facing the issue of private schools honestly, and they have not thought through the consequences of their policies in the state sector, approaching selection in an anarchic way. The Tories' determination to 'set up' Labour on the issue reflects both a crudity of tactics and the poverty of the Party's thinking on where the system as a whole is going.

To throw out calls for more grammar schools in the absence of a vigorous strategy for high-grade technical schools smacks of incoherence – all the more so since the public is lukewarm or negative when it comes to making local decisions about selective schools. As for technical education (though the subject has at least been included in the National Curriculum), claims that the need for specialist schools is being adequately met by a series of high-profile intitiatives, notably city technology colleges, are another example of self-deception.

Though welcome enough in themselves, statistically such schools are insignificant. Eight years after their launch in the White Paper 'Choice and Diversity' there are 15 CTCs out of a total of 3,500 secondary schools. Their cost – some fifty millions – is half as much as the Assisted Places Scheme. What is most characteristic about them explains why, despite recent claims of progress with the initiative, there will almost certainly not be many more. The schools were conceived as partnerships with industry, with local firms helping to meet initial costs. In an ideal world, a modern version of the schools endowed by merchants in the sixteenth or seventeenth century would be an ideal solution. Yet in contemporary Britain the notion is tinged with the besetting Tory sin of nostalgia.

The conditions under which the Merchant Taylors, Haberdashers' Aske, or other such schools were set up are somewhat different from those pertaining today. It may be reprehensible of private business and industry to leave what they see as basic education to the state but – huge corporate taxpayers that they are – they are unlikely in their majority to change the habits of a lifetime. There is every reason for business to be more engaged in industrial training and inter-active with secondary education, and a number of schemes (such as the Technical and Vocational Initiative) have successfully promoted this interaction. Yet to believe that business will become involved in the financing and running of our schools to any significant degree is to evade reality. To that extent CTCs are an example of educational romanticism on the Right. For the same reason it makes little sense to call, as the Prime Minister has, for a grammar school to be set up in every town on local initiative, to be funded partly by locally raised money.

Diversification in general, and the provision of technical schools especially, cannot be a random affair, left to the goodwill of this or that company or to the uncertainties of communal action. Even if it were successful, the call for more grammar schools in isolation from a determined policy to promote technical schools of equal prestige alongside them would bring us back to the old dilemmas of selection in a new form.

For once the answer really does have a lot to do with money. Equipping a technical school to a high specification is a costly business. Teachers are harder to find, and in a competitive employment market cost more too. So far efforts in this direction have been tentative (Heathrow Airport again), such as the release of extra funds to schools who pledge themselves to become centres of excellence in technology teaching. A more dynamic, ambitious and better-funded initiative is required. Whether they are based on existing comprehensives or whether they are new, free-standing structures, whether grant- or LEA-maintained, in smart suburbs or inner cities, Britain needs more urgently than ever what we never had after 1944: a network of superbly equipped, high-aiming technical schools that will attract talented and aspiring pupils and teachers alike.

In some cases it may be possible to split existing comprehensives (often inhumanly large) into two main streams, operating from the same campus. In others individual comprehensives could specialise (some already are). If it so falls out that in area after area we are left with a pattern of academic and technical schools, with entry by aptitude and flexible interchange of pupils as those aptitudes evolve and are manifested, who but the nostalgics of egalitarianism and bureaucratic order would object?

Chapter Nine

Higher Education

'I don't think one "comes down" from Jimmy's University.'

(*Look Back in Anger*, by John Osborne).

* * *

Of all the educational nightmares on the Right, where there are many, the worst would be to discover that the protests of the educational establishment at the Government's innovations had been nothing more than a feint. All the while they had been quietly converting the reforms to their own use, as guerrillas re-adapt captured weapons, and after seventeen years of a centrally directed campaign, the centre would wake up one morning to find itself out-gunned and surrounded.

The nightmare is not entirely paranoid. It is possible to imagine a scenario in which the Government's reforms would be bent to a quite different purpose. If the National Curriculum were to degenerate into a mishmash, national testing became a formality with 90 per cent of pupils performing 'satisfactorily or better', grant-maintained schools settled back into a cosy relationship with LEAs, A-levels were progressively diluted to conform to the requirements of the GCSE, and the number of pupils qualifying for higher education rose to the point where the flood gates gave way and degree courses became little more than extended sixth forms, then the Right would have engaged the battle and the egalitarians would have won. Our universities, the high ground of the system, would subside beneath the waves like so many drowned cathedrals.

Already in higher education there are people of no pronounced political persuasion who feel the nightmare coming on. 'The present system,' wrote Sir John Mason, the former Chancellor of the University of Manchester Institute of Science and Technology (UMIST), in his retirement speech, 'which allows any student with minimal qualifications to follow any course or mixture of courses without regard to intellectual or vocational quality, utility, social or economic need, and at the taxpayers' expense, is not sustainable . . .'

The legacy of the first great expansion of higher education in the sixties was mixed: it gave us more graduates, more dons, some ugly or indifferent buildings, and *The History Man*. Whatever one's views on the cultural consequences, for economic reasons if nothing else, it had to be done. There was no option of continuing to reserve university education to less than 3 per cent of those of an age to qualify, as had been the case in pre-war Britain, or to hold it down at 7 per cent, the level reached in 1962, the time of the Robbins Report which gave rise to the first great expansion. Fifteen years later that figure had almost doubled, and by the early nineties it had quadrupled to roughly a third of young people.

In other words we have gone from 219,000 full-time students in 1962 to 1,079,000 in 1995. Including all-comers (such as part-time students) brings a grand total of 1,700,000 – highly respectable by international standards, especially when it is remembered that the basis of comparison is frequently flawed, with some countries including nurses, for example, in the figures.

Now the numbers game is over. The issue today is not quantity but quality and purpose. For the moment a simple answer to the 'more means worse' theory would be that British higher education in the nineties is still seen as at least on a par with and often better than its foreign analogues. For the moment. It is important to be clear about the reasons for this relative – and fragile – success.

The single most striking fact about the British system of education is the contrast between the distinction of many of its universities and the poor quality of many of its schools. There are many explanations for our top-loaded system. One may simply be that the universities are by their nature more closely connected with the political players and decision-makers, and therefore better placed to influence policy. Another is that the middle and upper middle classes have a more direct interest in sustaining excellence in our universities than in our schools. One need look no further than the correspondence columns of *The Times*, MPs' postbags, or speeches in the House of Lords, to see that the prospect of change in the funding or organisation of the universities mobilizes the upper stratum of society to a far greater extent than any reforms affecting primary or secondary education.

People who showed little interest in the standards of schools they did not use, and who were disinclined to exert pressure either for better teachers or better resources, were more sensitive to what happened in the institutions of higher learning that their children progressed to after their independent schools. Here was a high-quality, generously funded state service, delivered free of charge (i.e. no tuition fees) to rich and poor alike, to which the social and moneyed elite (by whom its best institutions were disproportionately used) had become understandably attached. Of all the universal benefits available to the upper classes higher education is the only one for which no private substitute is available (outside our only independent institution, the University of Buckingham) and which no amount of money can buy.

It was all part of the unspoken British educational settlement. The psychology behind it – insofar as it was conscious – was not unreasonable. Having already dug deep into their pockets to keep their children out of maintained education, while simultaneously paying for the children of others through their taxes, when it came to higher education people felt no compunction about exploiting to the maximum the best the state could offer. You could purchase a place for a bright child at Eton, but not at Oxford – though it was by paying for it at Eton that you stood a better chance of securing the place at Oxford. That was (and to an extent still is) how the wheel turned. The fact that a high-quality service benefited those at the middle and lower levels of society was incidental, though a handy alibi for the continuation of a free system. So things have continued, more or less satisfactorily, for decades.

How long can the unspoken settlement in our universities last, and their prestige be maintained, now that a second wave of expansion has intervened? The first thing to remember is that the superiority of our system has always been relative to the shortcomings of others. To excel the French at higher education, for example, is no great achievement. Against the better judgment of both experts and politicians, successive French governments have been obliged for traditional reasons to maintain a mass, open-entry system which has reduced many of their universities to an over-crowded, under-resourced shambles. The super-elite *grandes écoles* are to some extent a substitute, though by that stage of the process the cream is so small in quantity and so highly refined that, while it is ideal for the confection of prime ministers and presidents, or top flight engineers and administrators, it cannot be put to more general use.

The second point to remember is that the quality of British higher education, with its much lower staff–student ratios, free tuition fees, freedom to move about the country, and student maintenance grants and loans, has been dearly bought: the average cost to the state per student is almost double that of France (£6,500 as against £3,500) and a third higher than Germany. Certainly our system is more efficient, with its three-year degrees, low drop-out rates and the rest. But to justify continuing that level of expenditure the achievements of the system need to be twice as good as the French and a third better than the Germans.

The third cloud is not so much on the horizon as over our heads. How long can we base good universities on indifferent schools? In an era of expansion the output of our universities will be related increasingly directly to the quality of what is taken in. And if that expansion has been under-funded (as seems to be the case) in a high-cost system, and if it was a mistake to designate polytechnics as universities (as can at least be argued), the consequences for everyone, from 'elite' backgrounds or otherwise, could be the same.

On present trends we risk a gradual subsidence into mass, inadequately funded higher education, of indifferent quality: a 'comprehensivisation' of the system. Were that to happen the best part of our education would go the way of the rest. Bleaker assessments suggest it has already happened: in the same retirement speech Sir John Mason said openly what many an academic privately thinks: 'The decision to expand higher education before attending to the schools was like adding an extra storey to a house with crumbling foundations.'

The strains are there to be seen: in library provision, in crammed lecture halls, in scarcity of accommodation, and crucially in staff–student ratios. In the early seventies in universities it was a luxurious 1:8 (in France the figure was 1:25, elsewhere around 1:20). Now that figure has risen to 1:12. In the former polytechnics, where most of the expansion has taken place, the rise has been even more dramatic: from 1:8 in 1979 to 1:19 in 1992/3, the increase entirely due to rising student numbers, since staff numbers have increased as well.

The scope for some tightening of the ratios was widely recognised. There was never any realistic possibility – or on some courses necessity – of maintaining some of the most generous ratios in the Western world. Nor has expansion been entirely on a shoestring: between 1979 and 1994 expenditure on universities doubled in real terms, from a billion and a half to more than five billion pounds. Yet whichever way you look at the figures the money spent on the average student has been falling.

The real trouble comes at the point of interaction between the perhaps too-easily-admitted student and the overloaded system. The effects of rising staff–student ratios and lower entrance qualifications are geometrical: the less intellectually ready students may be to follow a university course, the more contact-time is needed with tutors, where they exist. Under the present trend, students will get less. It is scarcely surprising to see our low drop-out rates edging up. We have reached the stage of decisions. If we wish to maintain the relative quality and efficiency of our universities there comes a moment when it has to be recognised that the slack in the system has been more than taken up.

The danger of over-stretching the capability of institutions to absorb extra students was not unforeseen when expansion was discussed in the mid-eighties. It would be a simple-minded Government who thought you could cram in more students indefinitely without risk to quality. (The hope was of course that standards in schools would rise in parallel.) Only market romantics seriously believed that, by a combination of belt-tightening, better management, better teaching with modern methods, and attracting private money and foreign students, the value of a University degree in a hugely expanded system could continue unimpaired.

There were other kinds of romantic: those who affected to believe (or still worse *did* believe) that the Treasury should simply find the money from the taxpayer, and that expenditure per pupil could continue at its previous high rate in a system tripled in size. Such people comprised a wide political spectrum, ranging from the liberal-left to the upper-class beneficiaries of a totally state-funded system. Here was another of those unlikely *de facto* alliances one stumbles across in British politics. Both leftist and patrician had a joint interest in letting expenditure rip – the only difference being that, if he had his way, the leftist would seek to recoup the money by raising the taxes paid by the patrician.

To sober-minded people on all sides of Parliament the solution to the financial problems of our universities has been obvious for some time, though such is our system that sobriety and politics are frequently incompatible. Open discussion of where the money was to come from was impossible during the entire period of expansion, and remains so till this day. To all intents and purposes Parliament has side-stepped the issue entirely.

The confrontational politics which had played their part in the failure to attack the roots of under-performance in our schools were again evident in the failure to make proper provision to uphold standards in universities. The least intelligent of political systems has produced a not notably intelligent solution for the financing of the higher education of the country's most intelligent young people: the solution being to go on cramming them in till the system was brimming to overflowing, and then stop.

The slightest reference to the funding needs of our universities is enough to set the Westminster tribes a-booing and a-yahooing. In the case of the late Sir Keith Joseph this was literally the case. When, with his compulsive honesty, he told a backbench meeting of Conservative MPs – already the butts of middle-class insurrection over the proposed scheme for student loans – that there might one day have to be some parental contribution to the cost of fees, desks were banged and loud interruptions made.

That, in effect, was the extent of the debate on the financial future of our higher education system in the parliamentary Conservative Party. When vice-chancellors contemplate their overflowing campuses and ask themselves where expansion went wrong they need do no more than picture that scene. There has since been a great deal of discussion outside Westminster, in think tanks and the like, much of it sensible, but no Secretary of State for Education has reverted to the theme. Academics are notoriously prone to what one of them once called the 'higher silliness'. In Parliament that same behaviour can disguise itself under the name of a great parliamentary tradition.

The reason MPs declined all rational discussion in the way they did was not necessarily because they were opposed in principle to parental or student contributions to fees, or failed to appreciate the damaging effects on universities of underfunding in the longer term. It was because they feared for their seats. The issue being politically delicate amongst the overwhelmingly middle-class beneficiaries of a free system, they knew that however sensible the solution, Labour would reject it. The iron law of our politics – that oppositions exist not to supply alternative policies but to make trouble for the Government – has limited and deformed debate on higher education even more than elsewhere.

The Labour position at the time was first to demand massive expansion, then, when it came, to claim that the Government was not providing the resources. They had no plans about how to meet the costs themselves and were not going to allow any new thinking on the matter on their own benches, any more than backbench Tory MPs were in the Government. An exception was the thoughtful and brave MP for Perry Barr, Jeff Rooker, Opposition spokesman for Higher Education and, financially, a highly literate politician. But when he issued a paper suggesting a graduate tax as the fairest means to ease the pains of expansion, he was sacked. Like Sir Keith, he had hinted at the truth and was duly punished.

The episode brought to mind a conversation I had previously had with the late and genuinely lamented John Smith on a similarly sensitive subject – mortgage tax relief – at a time when he was Shadow Chancellor of the Exchequer and Margaret Thatcher was still Prime Minister. Over a late-night drink we agreed that the system was an iniquitous and costly nonsense. When I asked (not totally seriously) why he didn't use his relative freedom as Shadow Chancellor to say so, he gave his impish grin and said: 'I will if she will.' The remark becomes all the more poignant when it is remembered that the cost of indiscriminate tax relief to rich and poor was then fuelling the housing boom to the tune of some £8 billion pounds annually – about double the cost of the whole of our higher education, and a sum which might more usefully have been spent on our schools. (It is a sad coda to the story that, as Opposition Leader, it was John Smith who sacked Jeff Rooker.)

As in so many other areas of economic discussion, when it comes to the question of the future of our universities the public is kept in a state of arrested development. Higher education, like the NHS, is a great British good. Everyone clamours for an expanded service as a matter of conscience, but no one wants to discuss the financial implications. So it was that millions of otherwise intelligent people – students, their parents, the parents of future students, not to speak of dons and vice-chancellors – were encouraged in the economically childlike belief that the universities could be indefinitely expanded and that the Government of the day would pick up the bill.

Almost a decade later, after three generations of students have suffered, Parliament is faced with the same problem as before: how to communicate to middle-class voters and their student progeny the stark inevitability of some kind of contributary system to the cost of fees. Following the report of the left-leaning Social Justice Commission under Sir Gordon Borrie the Labour Party appear to be coming round, privately at least, to Jeff Rooker's graduate tax, for which there are precedents abroad, and the Liberal Democrats are toying with a similar system. The Conservatives, having had their fingers painfully singed in the Joseph episode, are silent, though both the Government and many backbenchers are unlikely to be opposed on principle to such a solution.

So we have a situation where all sides of Parliament are tacitly agreed on the nature of the problem and the likely cure – though nothing is divulged to the public. To admit to cross-party agreement would be unthinkable. Instead an inquiry under Sir Ron Dearing has been established, which is clearly designed to edge the question out of public view till after the election: Labour, as delighted as the Government to be off the hook, has (unusually) agreed.

Had an inquiry been agreed seven years earlier, the beneficial effects of its not unpredictable recommendations in favour of a new source of finance would already have been visible on campus. As it is, all that is certain is that, should Labour be in power when Sir Ron Dearing reports, the Conservatives will use every trick in the book to embarrass the Government in the eyes of the middle classes, and so delay a solution further. Even if all goes unexpectedly smoothly it will be years before the finances of our higher education are placed on a secure basis.

The record of dons and vice-chancellors is hardly better. With the exception of Professor John Ashworth, till recently Director of The London School of Economics, Sir Derek Roberts, Professor of University College, London and a handful of others, the vice-chancellors, who had no electorate to fear, distinguished themselves neither by the firmness of their resolve nor by the realism of their prescriptions. Far from exercising their joint authority to call all sides to order and to appeal for a grown-up debate on the financial future of their institutions, they kept their heads well up in the clouds and their feet planted firmly on shifting sands.

Had the vice-chancellors come forward with serious plans for financing the expansion they collectively favoured, it would have been that much more difficult for Parliament to pursue the complicity of evasion that passed for debate. What happened was a grand passing of the buck, as the most intellectually distinguished group of men and women in the country acted like the most narrowly self-interested of pressure groups: they simply asked for more cash without any serious consideration of where it was to come from, and in airy disregard of competing priorities. Their recent threat to impose a student entrance levy was an obvious attempt to drive the Government into producing money they have not got; or, on a more charitable explanation, into imposing a full-scale system of graduate contributions to fees they are too squeamish to advocate themselves.

Even the House of Lords, free as it too is of electoral pressures, has contented itself largely with pious expressions of concern. The collective failure of leadership of our most venerable institutions – Parliament, the House of Lords, and the Universities – lends credence to the theory that Britain is indeed becoming a society of dysfunctional elites.

If the first great myth was that university expansion could be indefinitely financed by Government money, an even bigger example of self-delusion was the idea that more cash alone would protect and enhance the quality of the system: a crudely materialistic notion, yet one that has its defenders in our higher education, as in our schools.

Expansion was based on two premises that have been shown to be false: first that it was financially containable; second that rising standards in schools would provide a growing pool of ability for higher education. As the participation rate increased, it was thought, so would the qualifications of potential students as the reforms at secondary level brought forth their fruits. As noted, for their different reasons Right and Left were obliged to pretend that these fruits were ripening at the speed intended.

A recent study of the 1995 entry requirements by the University Council Admissions System (UCAS) in 'traditional' and 'new'

Universities (i.e. ex-polytchnics) does little to sustain hope that this is happening. The average A-level points needed to secure a place vary enormously between more demanding and more popular subjects. In traditional universities 21 points are needed to read English, business or media studies; for physics it is as low as 16. In former polytechnics the pattern is the same – though here the requirement for physics and mathematics falls to 10 and 9 respectively.

Since 9 points is the equivalent of three A-levels at DDE or less, it is permissible to wonder why pupils with such low attainments are accepted for a place at university, with the expense the British system involves, at all. The reason of course is that, simply to fill the available places, and to maintain the 'output' of higher education in the crucial fields of engineering, physics and mathematics, the universities are under pressure to accept whatever the schools provide.

To maintain that higher education should continue to expand even if it means accepting lower standards of inputs and outputs, and that in the humanities we should consciously work towards the American model of liberal arts colleges, is a mistaken view on many counts. It has the smell of defeatism about it, and leaves aside the important matter of the level of results the country is entitled to expect in return for our relatively costly system.

The academic community is not unaware of what is happening. Little has been said openly, with the honourable exception yet again of Sir John Mason. Commenting on a Ministerial complaint that some institutions award no third-class degrees or failures, he said: 'What did he expect? Given the decline in teaching standards, dilution of O-levels by GCSE and the consequent gap between GCSE and A-levels, where were the greatly increased numbers of able, highly motivated students to come from?'

Such outspokenness, albeit on retirement, is not the rule. In our universities, on the matter of standards in schools and the philosophies of education that determine them, corporate discretion rules. There is a public and private discourse, and the difference between them is stark. In the cloistered recesses of colleges there is much wailing and tearing of hair about semi-literate students and the low level of pre-university attainment in maths and physics, but the sound of these lamentations remains decently secluded.

Almost never – and certainly never collectively – are public doubts expressed in higher educational circles about the origins of under-performance at primary and secondary levels. The Moser Commission on Education of 1992, a privately funded enterprise, with its mild and muffled criticisms of the teaching profession, was the closest we have got. Which vice-chancellor, one wonders, will be the first to take a public stick to theorists of progressivism? If the left-leaning press, such as the *Guardian*, *Observer* and *Independent*, and now even the Labour Party, are beginning to look reality in the eye, why not those in charge of our universities?

Should individual dons break ranks, it is frequently to call for a fourth University year. This again is defeatism. The implication is that we should reconcile ourselves to low or indifferent standards in schools, and pursue the chimera of even higher expenditure per pupil in our universities to compensate for failure earlier on.

Those most directly concerned by under-achievement have failed to give a lead. One might have expected that calls for a root and branch inquiry into our primary and secondary failures should come most loudly from those who suffer most from their consequences, and who are intellectually best equipped to discuss causes and cures. No one has a more direct interest in getting the fundamentals right first time, rather than attempting correction in later years at enormously greater cost, and at the risk of turning further and higher education into remedial institutions. It is their own national and international reputation that stands to decline if nothing is done. Why not summon the joint resources of our universities to do it themselves? The impact of an objective report and practical recommendations from the highest intellectual body in the land could scarcely be ignored, and would make the party-political machinations of Parliament on education that much harder to sustain.

Sadly, fear of offending vested ideological interests makes it unlikely that such an inquiry will be forthcoming. No doubt vice-chancellors fear that to argue the toss over the doctrines in force in our schools could prove a jarring and 'divisive' business. In some of our more prestigious universities the preferred option seems to be to treat symptoms and not causes, by devising ever more tortuous means of increasing the share of comprehensive school pupils in their intake of students. So are our social consciences stilled while the educational roots of inequality remain untreated.

Despite such stratagems the chances of the non-privately educated pupil gaining admittance to elite institutions, far from improving with the years, have declined. A single statistic is suggestive of the extent of the regression. In 1970 59 per cent of students at Oxford University came from state or direct grant schools (45 per cent state, 14 per cent direct grant). Independent schools accounted for 38 per cent. In 1994 the figures were: state, 33 per cent, independent 44 per cent (the others were accounted for by different modes of entry). With every allowance made for the difficulty of comparison due to the unclear status of direct grant schools and the abolition of most grammar schools, and for natural sociological determinants, the securing of almost half the places by 7 per cent of the pool of talent is an eloquent symbol of what has been happening in our schools.

As a Minister, I once took part in a debate about education spending at the Oxford Union. Student loans were in prospect at the time. It was obvious before a word was spoken that I was going to be defeated, so there seemed nothing to lose by telling the truth. I told the assembled students that they should consider themselves fortunate to be attending one of the finest universities in the world, though if we had a serious system of state education a high percentage of my audience might not be there. My package of economic realities and social verities found the number of takers I had anticipated. In the vote, I lost spectacularly.

Inverted snobbery, social resentment and academic defeatism play their part in ensuring that the number of state school pupils at some of our most reputable universities remains restricted. The experiences of Nick Forbes, currently president of the Cambridge

Union, provide a startling insight into the nether world of educational Calibans to be found in some of our schools. The teachers at his North East comprehensive, he has said, did not know how to apply for Oxbridge entry, and were not inclined to find out: 'The headmaster had very strong views that Oxbridge was an awful, elitist place. When I wanted extra lessons to prepare me for the exam applicants can take in the sixth term, the teachers flatly refused to give them.' (The *Independent*, 28 March 1996).

As Minister of Higher Education, in each of the twenty-five universities I visited (polytechnics were still polytechnics at the time) I made a point of asking vice-chancellors or admission tutors about the ratio of state as opposed to privately educated students. The question provoked the mixture of defensiveness and embarrassment familiar to anyone conversant with the system. The average intake from private schools is 25 per cent, though figures vary greatly and, needless to say, broadly in line with the quality of the institution. (The proportions from the 153 remaining grammar schools were of course also high, a factor which helps to disguise the under-performance of the comprehensives.) Time and again I was assured that the universities were doing their best to correct the imbalance, and to ensure that applicants from state schools were given their full chance. From the frankest of the dons came a painful message:

> 'Put yourself in our place' was the tenor of these conversations. 'We are confronted by two potential students, of broadly similar academic qualifications, one comprehensive educated, the other from a private school. The shortcomings of many in the first category are often pitifully obvious. They write much less fluently and grammatically than their private school competitors. They are far less articulate. They have read much less round their subject, contenting themselves with their set books, and are generally less cultivated than they should be. They have less confidence, and as a result present themselves gauchely.
>
> 'If they are studying a foreign language they can't speak it too well, any more than their own. If they want to read

maths they have often been inadequately taught. We know from experience that, if we take the state-educated pupil, much time will be spent in preparatory work of one sort or another. In the case of the second, privately educated candidate we can move straight into the University syllabus.

'Try as we might we are not clairvoyants. There is a limit to how much time we can afford to spend examining the credentials of individual candidates. Given their problems of self-expression, written or oral, it is often hard to judge the intellectual potential of the ex-comprehensive pupil: they may be rough diamonds, they may be duds. The opposite can often be true of the privately schooled applicant: the polished manner and shimmering surface may conceal pastework underneath. If the judgement is that their potential is broadly similar, which are we to choose? The one who is ready to take on a university course, or the one who is not? To what extent do we turn ourselves into remedial institutions to make good the deficiencies of the schools? To what extent are we social improvers? What would be the consequences for the University as a whole, and the value of our degrees, if we adopted a semi-conscious policy of positive discrimination?

'Experience in going for the state-educated pupil can be highly positive. When we detect, on the basis of examination results, reports from schools, and from the brief time at our disposal for interview, that an applicant possesses a capable though raw intelligence, if we make the right choice he or she can flourish in the more demanding university environment and swiftly overtake his or her privately educated counterpart. But there are contrary cases, where we bend over backwards to favour the comprehensive applicant only to discover that years of poor teaching and a narrow culture have left an indelible mark. As in every human institution, the tendency is to play safe.'

One of the many subjects on which academics are wary of speaking their minds publicly, in cases where these minds do not coincide with conventional attitudes, is gender. In terms of female students there has been a twofold expansion in higher education. While the total number of students enrolled has doubled since 1980, the numbers of women within these totals rose by 176 per cent, from 303,000 to 835,000. Now 47 per cent of full-time undergraduates are female. The signs are that the numbers will rise further and women could soon be in a majority.

If it is true that the quality of higher education is subsiding following over-expansion, women seem likely to be more prominent amongst the victims than men. The reason they are more vulnerable relates to the higher numbers of women studying humanities courses. Definitions can be imprecise, but some idea of the disproportions between male and female students emerge from the following figures:

Thousands of full-time first degree students by subjects in further and higher education, 1993/4

Subject	**Males** (000s)	**Females** (000s)
Mathematical science:	32.9	10.8
Engineering and technology:	58.1	10.3
Languages:	14.9	34.2
Creative arts:	19.4	26.5
Education	2.2	5.8
Social sciences:	39.5	45.7

The picture is blurred in some areas (for example by the larger number of women studying biological science) but overall it is clear enough. If the system is in decline there would be no reason in principle why standards should fall more in the humanities than in the sciences. In practice, as seen in the 16–19 study by Sir Ron Dearing calling for better quality in A-level subjects such as English, and remembering that international comparisons of achievement are easier to make in the sciences than the arts and humanities, it is easy to see why this might be so.

The point is not to decry the growth in the proportion of women students, which is overdue. Nor is it to impugn their academic capabilities or achievements, which would be absurd. It is also possible that the proportion of women doing 'hard' subjects, such as maths, will increase as stereotypes and superannuated cultures break down and girls are encouraged to widen their ambitions in these areas from an early age: there is currently much discussion about whether or not single-sex schools, or segregated classes in the sciences, are the best way of promoting this.

Yet we start from where we are. The danger is that women who find themselves studying for what may be sub-standard humanities degrees on overcrowded and under-tutored courses will discover, when they emerge into the world, that their degrees have less value in the workplace than they had been led to believe. The same would be self-evidently true of men, but the number of disappointed women would be greater simply because there are more of them studying the courses in question.

Already many female graduates find themselves doing what is essentially secretarial work. From the graduate's viewpoint, doing work for which she feels (and may well be) intellectually over-qualified can be a frustrating experience. Should she *not* be over-qualified for her work the waste of national resources is immense: a three-year university degree is an expensive way of training secretaries.

The fact that these things remain unsaid, for pietistic reasons, does not make them less true. In plain language (not a speciality of the academic community), if standards in the humanities decline in the course of expansion, hundreds of thousands of women will have been sold a pup: an educational preparation for life less demanding than it should be and a job lower than their intelligence merits. Hardly a recipe for equality between the sexes. Discovering that male students had bought the same pup, though in smaller numbers, would be scant consolation.

The conclusion is simple: that if they have the true interests of women at heart, advocates of equality would be well advised to keep as close an eye on the quality of the education women are offered at university as on the numbers who enrol. For the first generations of women to benefit from a numerically equal system to emerge from higher education with high hopes, only to find that their degrees are not as highly valued by employers as they would like, and that the jobs they are offered are beneath their potential, would not be good for anyone, least of all men.

Fears that egalitarian values are seeping into higher education, to the detriment of male and female students alike, are borne out by the recent history of the polytechnics. When the question of renaming them as universities was under consideration I voiced my misgivings to Ministers. In effect I was told that the pressure for change had become irresistible, and that it was 'one of those ideas whose time had come'.

The first explanation I interpreted as meaning that the Government had lost the will to resist the pressure for parity of status from the polytechnic directors – an otherwise sober body of men and women who had done good work in making their institutions more efficient – and had thrown them the bone of university status as a reward for services rendered. 'An idea whose time has come' – a cloudy phrase at the best of times – I interpreted as a reluctance to argue the case logically, with me or anyone else.

It being one of those changes that is irreversible, there would seem little point in re-arguing the toss. The reason it was done is, however, of direct and continuing relevance to the education debate. If polytechnics go by the name of universities today it is not because of educational imperatives, but for reasons of social status: another example of how class-consciousness has decided educational policy. As a Minister overseeing the polytechnics who was unwilling to change their name, I was once offered a compromise: if the Government were reluctant to go the whole hog, could they call themselves poly-universities? My response was that this came uncomfortably close to someone adopting a double-barrelled name for less than compelling family reasons. Those who suspect that I am over-emphasising the 'status' incentive for change should contemplate the zeal with which the new Universities have thrown themselves into designing escutcheons and similar academic paraphernalia betokening the antique origins and unbroken traditions of institutions established in the sixties.

The polytechnics, of course had plausible arguments. In essence their position was that parents saw polytechnics as second-best and as a result they were not getting their fair share of ability. 'Parity of esteem' could not be attained by a change of culture, so it had to be promoted by a change of name. It is important to remember that this concern is peculiarly British: the Massachusetts Institute of Technology does not lose much sleep over not being a University to itself, nor does the fact that a first-rate French engineer studied at the prestigious École des Ponts et Chaussées in France cloud his career. Our polytechnics, though less elite institutions, should have felt sufficient confidence in themselves and their achievements not to worry about it either.

Calling all institutions of higher education universities is like calling all schools grammar schools. The implication would be that non-grammar schools carry an eternal stigma of shame. The fact that even a Tory Government gave in to insistent demands reflects the depth of our national reluctance to make educational distinctions where they are necessary. There is a clear and unavoidable difference between a university and an institution geared essentially to technology, commerce and industry, and to applied rather than to pure research. The fact that they will inevitably overlap at some points obscures but does not obliterate the difference. It is there, serves a practical function, and is worth preserving.

Problems about status are in the beholder's mind. The answer is to correct misperceptions at an earlier stage by giving greater attention, prestige and resources to technical education in all its forms. To surrender to false perceptions is not to correct what was falsely perceived, but to distort the reality to suit the misperception.

You do not make apples more like pears by giving them the

same label. If anything you underline the difference, because the labels will inspire distrust if they conflict with experience: bite an apple and it tastes different to a pear because it is its function in life to do so. Far better to stand one's ground and be oneself, and let the perception catch up with reality. The main distinction in the future might well be that a computer engineer from a former polytechnic secures a well-paid job quickly, whereas a graduate with an indifferent degree in the humanities from an indifferent traditional university languishes on the dole. Who is then the gentleman?

A thing is itself. A polytechnic is not a university. Whatever escutcheon you nail over the entrance, however immaculate the lawn which surrounds it, however devious and ingenious the circumlocutions we resort to, in the minds of millions of people, not least its own students, a polytechnic it will remain.

Three years ago, the country's second great leap forward in higher education in thirty years came to a jolting halt. There were predictable complaints, with cries that the 'pool of talent' had yet to be exhausted, yet it was the right decision. As we pause for breath, now is the time to ask questions about the nature and purpose of the system we have created.

Does it make sense to produce so few vocationally oriented graduates and so many in the liberal arts – the latter perhaps of less than imposing quality – at such enormous expense? Should not science and technology students receive some sort of premium, to increase their numbers? Ought not the emphasis of government spending per pupil switch from universities to schools, so as to shore up the house built on loose foundations?

Our political parties are in broad agreement on how to handle such questions: they have agreed to postpone asking them till after the next election.

Chapter Ten

Money

> A primary head told a visiting Minister that, to increase parental involvement in his school, he wanted to have a photographer permanently on hand to capture the 'moment of discovery' on children's faces. 'Of course,' he said, meaningfully, 'there would be resource implications.'

* * *

Battles on the financing of our schools are fought with the same ferocity we devote to their organisation and structure, the purpose of the spending receiving less attention. Sometimes those who demand more money for education are concurrently concerned with improving standards, though more often they harbour an instinctual belief, peculiar to education, that money alone can buy skills, knowledge and wisdom. The level of thinking is comparable with the belief that happiness can be bought with the proceeds of a win on the national lottery.

It is a fact that Government spending on schools has increased from £5 billion in 1979 to £16 billion in 1995, yet somehow the sum fails to impress. This is not surprising. There can be no 'true' figure for spending on schools, nor can any figure ever be adequate. Always there will be a feeling that if only the needs of each child could be individually met in every respect, that child's talents could be more fully exploited and his or her prospects and character improved. In the same way that the entire GNP of a nation could without difficulty be lavished on health care and social security, education too has an infinite moral claim on those resources. In neither case can demand ever be fully satisfied. And just as unlimited healthcare will always fail the patient at the moment of death, so it could be argued that education, at whatever level it is provided, is bound to be inadequate, if only because there can be no such thing as a fully educated person.

Definitions of the 'correct' rate of spending will therefore always be arbitrary: anyone can name a figure and anyone else can cap it or cut it. In Britain, where Government expenditure is decided on a piecemeal basis from year to year, the arbitrariness is increased. The three main criteria are demand, available cash, and the politics of the moment. The base-lines are mainly historical and jealously guarded. As a result the most important criterion – national priorities – intrudes only at the margin. To confuse everyone further, until a few years ago income and expenditure were debated in Parliament at different times of the year: something that no well-run household would ever consider.

In this way the annual expenditure round becomes an interdepartmental exercise in bargaining and gamesmanship. The game is one in which civil servants, Parliament and the press connive. 'Successful' Ministers are not necessarily those who succeed in establishing a claim to greater national priority: they are those who get more. They openly boast about what they have 'won' for their departments and are duly congratulated by their clientele in the House of Commons, or by the lobbyists for the cause in question.

The process of allocating the public's money back to itself seems designed to invest what should be a stern adjudication between conflicting priorities with a distracting mystique. Hence our budget ritual – a peculiarly British occasion with its flummery and tradition – where an expectant populace waits to see what is handed down to it from above, like subjects waiting for Maundy money from a gracious sovereign. A 'clever' budget is one that persuades people that they are getting more services for less taxes, and budget packages are artfully studded with eye-catching measures to impress the impressionable. In the entire process, much depends on the credulity of the public.

As the lobby system becomes ever more sophisticated the temptation for governments to be all things to all men will increase accordingly – another game which the British parliamentary system is well designed to play. Any suggestion that fundamental spending priorities should be reviewed in the light of the nation's long-term needs is seen as an unacceptable threat to the day-to-day smooth running of the system. In practice there can be sensible shifts of priorities over time from one area to another, though such are the inhibitions against coming clean about what they are doing that governments are precluded from claiming credit for behaving in an enlightened manner.

After the collapse of the Berlin Wall I made a speech at the Royal Institute of International Affairs, entitled the 'Penalties of Victory'. My theme was that the Cold War had been a second 'great game' for the British, in which Governments of the Left and Right had performed creditably, from the Berlin airlift to the fall of the Wall. In terms of perpetuating our international prestige the whole business had been a godsend. However, now that the 'great game' was over the fundamental weaknesses of our society and economy would show through more clearly and painfully.

In terms of public finance my conclusion was that our spending priorities should henceforth be adjusted, notably between defence and education. The diplomats and generals present blinked a little when I suggested that nurseries should be part of our post-Cold War global strategy, though by and large they saw and agreed with the point.

A glance at the evolution of expenditure in these two fields in the ensuing years is instructive:

Expenditure on defence and education as a proportion of public spending in 1988 and 1995:

	Defence (%)	**Education (%)**
1988:	10.7	12.3
1995:	7	11.9

The pattern therefore has been a reduction of over a third in the proportion of our spending going to national defence, while educational spending has claimed a roughly static proportion of a growing budget. (The biggest increases went inevitably to social security.) The argument, popular on the Left, that Britain's problem is that we spend too much on defence and not enough on education, though historically valid, has therefore been overtaken by events. No doubt it could be argued that we could cut defence more. Leaving aside security and employment implications, which is to leave aside a great deal, even if new and severe cuts were made, defence now accounts for so little of our national spending that the savings would be of decreasing value.

Even if new money were to become miraculously available, Chancellors of the Exchequer of the Right or Left would be instinctively wary about devoting it to education, rather than to other fields. Smaller classes, for example, are pointless if teaching methods are suspect. An increase in health spending, on the other hand, is consistently at the top of most people's agendas in polls and surveys, and has more practical appeal. The results of greater investment are more visible more quickly, and – unlike schools – everyone stands to benefit in an immediate, material way. In a rational world the public could be persuaded that our future levels of health care will depend increasingly directly on the level of attainment in our schools, as international competition grows. But that is rarely the world politicians work in.

A way round this problem would be hypothecated taxation, which is to say that revenues collected from a given tax should be devoted to one end and no other. In education, for example, people might be more easily persuaded to give it the priority it deserves if they felt the taxes they paid went directly to schools. The idea is not novel, and has featured in the argument about the payment of taxes for defence by conscientious objectors, but it has been given a new spin by a pamphlet published by the independent think-tank Demos: 'Reconnecting Taxation'. The Liberal-Democrat campaign for a 'penny for education' (such are our levels of economic literacy that there are voters who believe this to mean a penny a week, or a year) and certain remarks by

Opposition economic spokesmen have also given new currency to an old debate.

The attractions of hypothecation are as evident as the difficulties are obvious. If tax demands came in portions – 5 pence in the pound for education, 7 for health, 9 for social security – people would see more directly how much they were getting for what they were paying. Yet this would by no means resolve the question of priorities: a parent with a child at school might support an extra penny to reduce class sizes; a pensioner nervous about a heart condition would be keener to spend the extra penny on reducing hospital waiting lists.

A further objection, voiced by the Institute of Fiscal Studies, is that even though hypothecated taxes already exist in the case of National Insurance contributions, this has not prevented successive governments from adapting their policy choices to the needs of the moment. The fact that so few people understand how the NIC system works is not a good augury for a more general system of hypothecation. In the words of the Institute it might 'mislead taxpayers rather than expand democracy'.

In the case of education the risks of hypothecation would be higher: here, more than anywhere else, it is possible to spend large amounts of money to little avail. It would be a bold individual who claimed that the fact that education expenditure has increased by 45 per cent since 1979 has pushed standards up by an equivalent percentage. Quite apart from the question of whether more direct taxation is desirable, or whether it would be counter-productive in economic terms, this is the major objection to the Liberal-Democrats' policy. They propose putting more money into our schools but have no parallel policies to ensure that more money will produce higher standards. All one could be sure of is that there would be further demands for more pennies.

As we feel around in the dark for the 'correct' level of spending on schools, international comparisons assume a more prominent role than in other areas. Instantly we find ourselves bumping up against walls and hastily recoiling. The ease with which international statistics can be manipulated in education is greater than elsewhere. A classic example was contained in a Department for Education and Employment press release in April 1995 commenting on an OECD report, claiming that the UK spends more on education than Germany. Closer inspection revealed that we spent more than Germany as a proportion of our public expenditure.

That too might seem impressive – until you reflect that the public expenditure of Germany, a richer country than ours, is higher too. The message could therefore be construed as being the opposite to the one the Government intended: in a rational world a poorer country would invest more money than a rich one on its education, in order to catch up.

The same press release claims that spending on primary and secondary schools as a proportion of GDP per head is above the OECD average and amongst the highest in Europe. Again, seen in isolation the claim makes little sense: our GDP per head is at the lower end of the European scale, so the same objection applies. All this leaves aside the fact that in the judgment of HMI the efficiency of our primary and secondary schools in terms of results is highly suspect. It follows that we could be in a position where not only are we spending less than we should to compete with other countries, but we may be putting our money into schools that are, on average, worse than theirs. The return on the investment would therefore be smaller. How much would it be worth investing in the primary school history lesson described in an earlier chapter?

Nevertheless we are forced to fall back on the available international statistics, since they are all that we have. The picture, inevitably, is mixed. In 1992, the latest year for which comparative figures are available (*Education at a Glance*, OECD, 1995), Britain spent 11.3 per cent of its total public expenditure on all levels of education. This put us just below the average. In terms of expenditure as a percentage of GDP we also come out on the low side at 4.1 per cent, though as noted this means we are above Germany, with its higher GDP. As a whole the OECD countries spend 6.1 per cent of their collective GDP on education, though again there are qualifications to be made: the disparities between countries are smaller than they appear when private spending is taken into account.

In spending per pupil expressed in terms of US dollars we are more generous to our primary school pupils than France and Germany (UK: $1,940; France: $1,800; Germany: $1,850.). On secondary pupils we spend more than Germany but less than France: (UK: $2,730; France: $3,380: Germany: $2,650). On tertiary education we are by far the most lavish: (UK: $6,450; France: $3,580; Germany: $4,070). And on nursery education we languish close to the bottom (UK $1,860; France $2,630; Germany $3,350).

It is important to see these raw figures in the context of educational policies as a whole. An overall assessment which has the ring of objectivity comes from the non-political Public Finance Foundation, whose report on education and training appeared in 1994. It concluded that, while public spending was by no means the highest in European and OECD terms, it was within 'the same broad range'. What marked us out from others in our post-war policies was:

(1) Higher spending on a relatively small number of students in higher education compared to schools, and higher private spending on independent schools;
(2) National policy focused on inputs to education (staff, buildings, organisation) rather than educational outcomes;
(3) the curriculum and teaching methods have traditionally been left largely to the profession;
(4) low priority for vocational education and industrial training;
(5) a relatively low proportion of pupils achieving a secondary qualification.

Many of these shortcomings are being addressed, for example, vocational training, though not always with the urgency they merit. In terms of the amount of resources we should devote to education in the future, four conclusions seem in order:

(1) Our spending policies should not be aimed at 'adequacy', or at catching up with other countries. We should aim to outpace them.
(2) The investment of more money, especially at nursery and secondary level, would not make us seem profligate in GDP terms.
(3) There are identifiable areas in which more spending, coupled with a change in teaching methods, could well increase quality, e.g. smaller classes.
(4) There are specific national and historical circumstances which may involve greater expenditure if we are to overtake others. Above all this applies to the cost of desegregating the system.

Looked at historically, the question of what proportion of the nation's wealth it would be wise for Britain to invest in education, if hard to put an exact figure on, becomes easy to define: it is the amount the higher echelons of society would spend on state schools if their own children attended them. It needs little imagination to conclude that, whatever that figure would be, it would be more than it is at present.

If the question is asked: how would we raise the money in a country that is already in debt? The answer could be said to be equally simple: in the same way that individuals show astonishing resourcefulness and readiness to make sacrifices when it comes to buying high-quality schooling for their children, so 'top people' would exert their influence to the maximum to ensure that budget priorities were adjusted. If savings had to be made elsewhere to provide free schooling of high quality to everyone on demand, so be it.

Politically a shift of national resources would depend crucially on presentation. What is needed is a new deal with the educational establishment. The government of the day would be buying out old attitudes and practices. The message to the profession would be simple: no change of culture in our schools, no new money. Without the abandonment of failed teaching methods and the accelerated diversification of our schools, the benefits of desegregating the state/private system would scarcely be worth the trouble and expense.

Would the public support such a stance? It may be optimistic to say so but it seems possible that there is a bigger market for realism and radical action than the quality of our current debate suggests. The insecurity mentioned in Chapter 1 is making the electorate more open to honest assessments about our prospects and weaknesses. The pressures of competition, combined with a dawning realisation that there is something fundamentally wrong with the structures and methods of our schools, could make it easier to put to the public measures which might have been impossible before. Making increased investment in education contingent on reform, while unlikely to be welcome to all teachers, would be entirely comprehensible to the man in the street. It is not necessary to be either an educationalist or an economist to understand that feeding higher-octane petrol into a faulty or poorly designed engine will not make the car go faster.

As for the sacrifices, the notion that if we wish to increase investment in one field spending must be adjusted accordingly in another is no longer a political taboo, as both main parties have foresworn major increases in direct taxation. Recently for example the Shadow Chancellor, Gordon Brown, suggested the abolition of child benefit from sixteen to eighteen and the investment of the savings, some £700 million, in training and education; a modest step, yet in the light of Labour's previous stance – that they favoured the retention of child benefit for all *plus* more spending on education – also a small miracle.

The terms of the package to be put to the educational establishment and to the public might be as follows:

Teachers

The first aim of higher spending would be to enhance the quality and numbers of the teaching staff. On numbers, staff–pupil ratios of the kind enjoyed by private schools would be as unrealistic for British state schools as they would be on the Continent. At the very least levels of staffing in secondary schools (18:1) must be maintained, and an improvement made in primary schools (currently 25:1, but with many over 30). Redeployment of staff from better-served to ill-served schools could mitigate the cost, estimated by the National Foundation for Educational Research at £130 million.

To secure better quality, it would be necessary to raise salaries overall. The cost to the Exchequer of, say, a 10 per cent rise in pay (about 7 per cent above inflation) would be of the order of a billion pounds. In maths, physics and technology, the existing differentials may have to be increased. Without agreement to higher differentials there would be no general increase. The replacement of national by local pay – another practice that it is time to buy out – would also be part of the bargain.

Nurseries

The Government's scheme for nursery vouchers for four-year-olds- involves £165 million of 'new money', over and above the £565 million already spent by local authorities on early learning. The cost of a full-scale system of nursery education from three to five has been put at over a billion pounds. The extra cost would therefore be in the order of £500 million.

Technical schools

The cost of a national network of well-equipped schools specializing in technology is hard to predict. Provision in new schools, especially in inner-city areas, would need to be generous to change a culture of anti-industrialism and low achievement. They would be beacons of hope, schools where people actually wanted to send their children, and where children, seeing the relevance of their studies to their prospects, would be happier to go.

On the rough and ready basis that £50 million was needed (topped up by industry) to set up and equip fifteen CTCs, a billion pounds injected into existing schools could serve to convert many into high-grade centres of technology.

A new Open Sector of independent schools

The cost of desegregating the system has been discussed. A working figure would be of the order of a billion pounds.

The total cost of such measures would be in the order of £5

billion pounds annually – the equivalent of 3p on income tax. If I leave out of the discussion the option of raising direct taxes it is for two main reasons: first, higher taxes could damage the economy; second, every interest group in the country could mount a case for similar treatment. Better on all counts to force the country to face a debate over priorities, in which the need for sacrifices would bring to the fore the purposes of the extra spending.

Transfers of resources
The switch of public expenditure would be of the order of 2 per cent. The cost would have to be borne by those best placed to bear it. The following are illustrative examples of where the savings might come from:

Taxing child benefit: £1,300 million.

A progressive run-down of mortgage tax relief: £3,000 million.

VAT extensions to books, newspapers and magazines: £1,200 million.

The yield from a graduate tax would depend on the rate and conditions, and would be spent directly in the universities.

What would be the cost of inaction to our economy and culture? By definition it is incalculable, but should not be over-dramatised. As Adam Smith said, there is a deal of ruin in a nation, and we are nowhere near ruin. Economically the short-term portents for Britain can be made to appear good, relative to others. It depends on one's readiness to think short-term, and on the level of one's aspirations. Like others in Europe we find ourselves immersed without warning in the icy, uncharted waters of a post-Cold War, technology-led global economy. As a matter of simple prudence one might have thought that we would invest in education, as in times of great international uncertainty we once defence. If nothing is done, and the global economy turns out to be as threatening to our long-term interests as it looks, despite all Britain's historical advantages what is already a second-rate country, educationally speaking, will sink to the status of a third-rate power.

Culturally, if our aspirations are on a par with the current achievements of our schools, then there isn't a problem, and we can rest contented. We have the education we want and deserve.

Chapter Eleven

Conclusion

'The trouble with Britain is that it does not have a plot.'
(Frederic Raphael, novelist)

* * *

'What have educated people ever done for this country?' The speaker was Margaret Thatcher, the place Ten Downing Street, the occasion a row between her and myself. We had been discussing the Broadcasting Bill. In arguing against the Bill, which in its original form planned to sell off TV franchises to the highest bidder irrespective of the quality of the programmes, I had told her that I failed to see how she could make speeches about the need to raise standards of education in the inner cities and the importance of spiritual values, while simultaneously selling off TV channels to the merchants of mediocrity and worse.

I could see that the argument had made a dent. As was normal when this happened, the last thing she was going to do was to admit it. Asking what educated people had ever done for the country was a typically tangential response, designed to switch the battle to a new front, and to spare her the pain of appearing to agree that, in some small part, she might have been mistaken.

In the sense that she meant it, it was a fair point. She was not of course questioning the utility of education as such. 'Educated people' was her code for the left-liberal establishment which she not unreasonably saw as having damaged the country by conniving in the dilution of standards. Had I not been primarily concerned with securing changes to the Bill (and she later relented to the extent of introducing a quality threshold for bids) it would have been entertaining to turn the question back on her.

What were educated Conservatives who cocooned themselves and their children in private schools doing for the country either, I might have asked? Where was their sense of patriotism? It is not hard to imagine her reaction. She would have affected indignation that I should make the comparison, called me a socialist, and found some way of switching the conversation. Whether that point too would have registered is doubtful, though you never quite knew. Sometimes she would reject an idea vehemently only to reproduce it herself at a later date, with all the force of revealed truth, as her own.

The idea that there might be any contradiction between patriotism and private schools would have come as a shock to her. On the thorny issue of the national interest versus choice and the market Conservatives are in a philosophical hole. There has been a good deal of non-thinking on the subject. The problem is most glaring in economics. Tories who trumpet their belief in their country and at the same time in the infallibility of market mechanisms find themselves in a stange position: they are both arch-patriots and arch-internationalists. Anti-Europeans are in an especially ambiguous position: when BMW take over Rover, the last British-owned mass-produced car firm, are they to denounce the economic imperialism of the Germans, or hail the immaculate benefactions of the market for saving a once great British enterprise from extinction?

The question of private education, being in the cultural domain, is more complex. Independent schools are free institutions operating within a free country (the theory goes) and we are all at liberty to decide how we spend our money – on the important assumption that we have it in the necessary quantity. Yet private schools are not the educational equivalent of Harrods or Peter Jones: the choice of an education for one's children has rather greater implications than the choice of a lampshade for one's drawing room.

What market-minded patriots are reluctant to recognise is that in a modern democracy independent schools cannot function as a nation apart, an educational state within a state which bases itself unashamedly on self, and group interest. Certainly their academic achievements are something to be proud of, and they have produced many brilliant individuals. Yet it is hard to see them as repositories of patriotism. It is a strange kind of patriot who wants the least possible contact with his fellow citizens, who loves his country yet disdains the company of his countrymen, and would be appalled at the thought of his children sharing their schools.

Much of the nationalist braggadocio in our press and politics, it will be noted, comes from people who have been insulated from their earliest years from the nation in question. The same people who swear to defend our sovereignty watch over the autonomy of their schools as they would the frontiers of a nation. In the unlikely event of a challenge to their existence or independence they would protect them with all the ferocity they would otherwise reserve for the defence of the realm. Which is natural to the extent that it pleases the more romantic amongst them to confuse their schools with the nation.

In the more hierarchical society of the past there was no problem about such attitudes. Physically separate and socially exclusive, public schools were nevertheless an organic part of the nation, in a feudal sense, and were seen as its finest expression. It was accepted without question that their purpose was to produce a ruling caste: the better the schools, therefore, the better for the country. Wars were won and the empire governed under the leadership of an elite educated to a standard not available to others. In more democratic times, identifying the national interest with that of a moneyed and social caste is neither possible nor desirable.

To call all parents who send their children to private schools unpatriotic would be absurd. As this book has sought to demonstrate, theirs is not simply a free but a rational choice. Nor of course is there any reason why users of private schools should be patriots at all, if only because patriotism cannot be *de rigueur* in a free country. If they felt a justification were needed in terms of the national weal, they could claim that by educating their children to the highest level attainable out of their own pockets they were doing the best for their country, as well as for themselves, and saving the Exchequer tens of thousands of pounds in the process. Or they could reject the question entirely and say that where they send their children to school is their own damned business.

What they cannot claim is that the choice they make for their children has no implications for the education of others. And should they regard themselves as both thinking people and patriots they would be obliged to reflect, in all honesty, about the consequences of a segregated system for the welfare of a country whose interests they see as close to their hearts. As they spurn – for understandable reasons – the schooling most people are forced to accept, at the very least such people must ask themselves where, educationally speaking, the nation is going?

Some may think this book too pessimistic about the condition of our schools. From experience I would guess that they will include a fair number of people who, while insisting that excellence is widespread in the state sector, do not avail themselves of it in the case of their own children. To such the answer can be only a smile.

More sincere critics deserve a more serious response. Education being a culture, many of my judgments are necessarily subjective, and what the jargon calls 'value-based'. So too are those of others, whose conflicting judgments it might be hard to disprove for the very reason that they may be based on different values. Yet in these shifting sands there is one fixed point. Suppose that things are better than I represent them in the state sector, that our political parties are converging in a joint effort to raise standards, and that in time more progress will be made. What is the conclusion? Are we to believe that independent education will decline and wither away? And if it does not, will there not always be a ceiling above which it will be impossible to raise standards for all in a segregated system?

The real pessimists, it seems to me, are those who, perhaps unconsciously, have reconciled themselves to the existence of that ceiling. To restrict our ambitions to doing what we can within 'the limits of the possible' goes beyond pessimism to covert defeatism. Is there not a tinge of national despair in such a stance? Given the growing importance of education in all aspects of our lives these attitudes appear to rest on an assumption that we are destined for relative decline, not simply in size or influence, but in the quality of our national life.

There is no lack of wider grounds for pessimism, if that is the mood. The notion that governments can determine by their actions the levels of achievement in schools is itself an oversimplification. Education is not a branch of the state like any other. Ultimately our schools are not in the government's hands, any more than broadcasting standards, or the flourishing or otherwise of the arts. Everything that matters – teaching styles, syllabuses, examination grades, the philosophy that drives the system – are, in thc last resort, outside the state's province. Ministers can goad, exhort, proffer incentives and punishments and manipulate things as best they can, but in the end they cannot decide. Even if their efforts at reform are well directed, as the journalist and cultural critic Bryan Appleyard has remarked, reforming education can be like trying to disperse a fog with a hand grenade: after the flash and the thunder, the fog creeps back.

The case for pessimism can be taken further. There does not *have* to be a solution to anything, and perhaps there is no solution to the problem of mediocre schools in mass societies? Different countries perform more or less well in their different cultures, but no one appears to have resolved this central dilemma. Starting as we do with a backward, two-tier system based on class obsessions rather than educational imperatives, why should we?

The most cogent reasons for restraining our hopes for education were voiced by the Spanish writer and historian Ortega Y Gasset (1883–1955). A liberal who opposed dictatorship, he nevertheless had few illusions about the democratic society he was attempting to promote in his country, and adhered to a nineteenth-century view of elitism. The modern world, he believed, expected far too much from its schools. In his *Mission of the University* (1944) he denounced what he saw as the myths that the battle of Waterloo had been won on the playing fields of Eton, and that the German victory over France in 1870 was the victory of the Prussian schoolmaster and the German Professor, and went on:

> These clichés rest upon a fundamental error which we shall simply have to get out of our heads. It consists in supposing that nations are great *because* their schools are good . . . It ascribes to the school a force it neither has nor can have . . . Certainly *when* a nation is great, so will be its schools.
>
> The school, when it is truly a functioning organ of the nation, depends far more on the atmosphere of national culture in which it is immersed than it does on the pedagogical atmosphere created artificially within it.

The message – that a country gets the schools it deserves – is not encouraging. If it is true, then Britain is faced with not just one chicken-and-egg enigma, but two. First, how do we raise standards in schools the most powerful and often best-educated people boycott precisely because of their low standards? And second, how can a once great country ever have a great system of education when it is not as great as it was? The pessimist's answer would be a despairing shrug. Mediocre country, mediocre schools.

If pessimism is the order of the day – and Ortega Y Gasset was one of the most profound pessimists of the twentieth century – then his are the most convincing grounds for resignation and inaction. If external cultural factors are all-determining, unless it is to keep our schools from the edge of the abyss, what is the point of striving overmuch to improve things? Yet such is human nature that, while having no ready answer to his dismal logic, we nevertheless have an urge to prove him wrong.

One reason for hope in Britain is that not a few Heads of private schools are beginning to think beyond the confines of their institutions. They are no longer the autocrats and blinkered figures of popular imagination. They know and care more about what happens in society as a whole than once they did, and are less inclined to close themselves off in their sphere of privilege. Nor is their more clear-eyed assessment of where we stand the product of guilt or of 'caring' postures.

Such people are aware that they have a duty to the country, as well as to themselves: that they are independent institutions with national responsibilities. For them it is not enough for private schools to expand and flourish in a two-nation system, since the logic of such attitudes would come dangerously close to *la politique du pire*: the worse things are in the state sector, the better for us.

They understand that, in a modern society, there is a limit on how long a part can thrive in isolation from the whole. What future can there be for the products of their schools in a country which, seen overall and in relation to its potential, is an educational failure? Where does that leave those who are schooled above the norm? If they work in the media will they find it rewarding to play down to the tastes of a sub-educated society, and make easy money out of ignorance and credulity? In some cases the answer will be an insouciant 'Yes, no problem'. Yet there are many talented people in broadcasting, journalism, or film-making who dream of doing more ambitious work than the cultural levels of their audiences allow.

If they are in publishing, where the healthiness of the bottom line is increasingly in inverse proportion to the demands made on the reader's intelligence, the same frustrations will apply. If they are politicians they may well be taken aback by the level of economic literacy they encounter when trying to put across the simplest argument. (After a discussion about the importance of industrial competitiveness in my constituency, just when I thought I had registered a point, a youngish, middle-class woman blurted out what she had clearly been thinking all the time: 'Why don't we just let the Japanese get on with making the cars, if they're so good at it, while we do what *we're* good at, which is caring?')

If they find themselves in a profession which takes them to other countries, might they not be struck by the relative freedom from social and intellectual contortions they encounter, and decide, as many of our best artists and writers have done, to live abroad? And if they stay at home, finding Britain a convenient base of operations despite everything, will they one day find themselves behaving like the internal émigrés mentioned in the first chapter? Secluded in their circle and in their homes, behind locks and grilles, as they try to seal themselves off, culturally and physically, from a marauding underclass? And even when more and more police are recruited and more malefactors are caught, will they feel content to watch prison after new prison overflowing with criminals, some of them evil, many more unemployable: unskilled, semi-literate Morlocks, articulate only in resentment, on whom society has given up in their school years, and who have given up on society in their turn?

If, in the course of this book, I have not emphasized enough the socially divisive effects of our segregationist culture of education, it is not because I do not deplore them as much as anyone: it is simply that it has been done before, *ad nauseam*. One should beware of inflaming emotions with which the country is overburdened, such as social malice, when what is needed is a clearer concentration on the educational roots of unequal opportunity. As for hierarchical stances and pretensions, they are scarcely worth attacking: all snobbery is vulgarity of the soul, and those whom it afflicts deserve our pity.

Inverted snobbery is more typical of the English condition in the late twentieth century, and far more damaging. Many people who have enjoyed a first-rate education waste a lot of their time and their talents, and much emotional energy, in expiation. Should they find themselves in influential positions, their compensatory gestures and postures are a touching spectacle. Watching them incline themselves before mass taste, one is reminded of penitents pleading for absolution.

Where else but Britain will you find ex-public schoolboys lampooning, in impeccable English, the teaching of grammar as a pointless pursuit? Where else in Europe is the fear amongst cultivated people of saying or writing something that might be considered 'inaccessible', 'exclusive', or 'divisive' so apparent? And where else does one find such anxiety to go with the tide, so many nervous genuflections and breast-crossings before the icons of popular culture? A simulacrum of democracy is necessary only for those who do not feel democracy in their bones.

In all modern societies there are artists or politicians whose dominant concern is to ingratiate themselves with what they clearly perceive as the masses, yet few can match the educated Englishman in his anxiety to please. Cultural self-abasement is the most distressing of perversions. Reflecting on its educational origins in England is enough to turn a man against the system.

'Britain lacks a vision' is a frequent complaint. The obvious answer is that visions are not the British style. Nevertheless, in the sense that we find it increasingly hard to read the map of the future, and to see how we shall feature, the complainers are right – though notoriously short on suggestions as to what 'a vision for Britain' might consist of.

If asked to define its essential elements there would be wide agreement. Whatever it is, our 'vision' must increase our pride in ourselves and be an antidote to intimations of decline. It must suggest ways of improving the nation's prosperity without being purely materialistic. It must engage the imagination and focus effort, without encouraging the belief that visions can be conceived and implemented by governments alone. Visions, like consciences, can also be expensive: the benefits must therefore be visible within a reasonable time, to justify the sacrifices.

Any 'vision for Britain' that did not include at its core the aspiration towards a world-class system of education open to all, and the practical means of achieving it, would be political vapour.

APPENDIX

An Educational Correspondence

GEORGE WALDEN, C.M.G., M.P.

HOUSE OF COMMONS
LONDON SW1A 0AA

Rt. Hon. John Major, MP
Prime Minister
10 Downing Street
London SW1

17th January 1995

Dear Prime Minister,

I am sending you the enclosed evidence of interest in the private, former Direct Grant sector, in rejoining the state sector because I believe it could be important for your educational policies. As you know such schools are a symbol of our national educational impasse: first-rate schools forced into the private sector in the years of comprehensivisation.

Coaxing them back into the state sector would be a great coup: a sign of the reversal of the tide, a boost to Grant Maintained status, proof that Conservatives want to open up opportunity to our unseen reserves of talent, and the sort of break-through in the public-private log jam you are seeking in many of your policies. The social symbolism speaks for itself. It would be that rare thing in politics – something that no-one could oppose!

A positive policy on private schools would have far more electoral appeal than Labour's policy of penalising them. I suspect Mr Blair understands this. One day he might even get round to something on the lines of my proposal. If ever he does, he would reap the electoral benefits.

The Assisted Places Scheme and Grant Maintained schools go some way towards alleviating the problem, but not far enough. The APS has a condescending "scholarship boy" feel to it, and there are too many cases of relatively well-off people being subsidised by those poorer than themselves. Opening up some of the former Direct Grant schools to all the talents *as of right* would be something different. As for GM schools, the flood has slowed to a trickle, and not all of them will use their funds for improving teaching, rather than facilities.

I am not starry-eyed enough to think that Eton would be first in the queue, or ever in the queue. But you yourself speak of the need for incremental policies. If some schools moved, other former Direct Grant Schools driven into the private sector might follow. When I discussed the idea some time ago with my own former Direct Grant school in London, they showed interest.

I see the problems and could write a long list of objections, not least financial, but am confident that others will do that for me. With sufficient imagination, they can be overcome. Nor am I innocent enough to suppose that our colleagues would be unanimously overjoyed. But whatever their traditionalist reservations, they would find it hard to object in public.

One thing is certain, and it is what inspires me to write this letter: though there can be improvements, there will never be a high quality state education system in Britain while the richest and most influential 7% opt for the private sector. They simply do not have the personal motivation to change things. Consequently Britain will remain a second-class country educationally, and therefore economically and culturally. The primitive social divisions and resentments manifested in our politics will also be perpetuated.

I have written articles and spoken in the Commons on the theme (enclosed). I do hope you can look into it.

Yours ever,

10 DOWNING STREET
LONDON SW1A 2AA

THE PRIME MINISTER

20 February 1995

Dear George,

Thank you for your letter of 17 January, enclosing a letter dated 9 January from Dr G M Stephen, High Master of Manchester Grammar School, together with articles on the theme of independent schools, such as Manchester Grammar and other former direct grant schools, being coaxed back into the state sector of education.

I find your thesis interesting and stimulating. You acknowledge the problems, not least financial. We certainly wish to see a public sector of education which is second to none. It is to this end that our education policies are working; and I believe there is plenty of room for debate on how further improvements might be achieved.

As you know, the last Education Act provided for independent promoters to propose to set up new grant-maintained schools, and this is the means by which independent schools can apply to join the GM sector. You will of course also be aware that it has been possible since 1944 for independent schools to apply to join the LEA-maintained sector as voluntary schools.

All such proposals will go before Gillian Shephard for decision. It is in the nature of her statutory role that she has to adopt a neutral stance towards proposals or pending proposals. Otherwise she could prejudice her eventual decision. Gillian considers proposals on their merits against a number of criteria, including whether the proposals contribute to increasing choice and diversity and enhancing the quality of education in the area, as well as the extent to which there is a need for additional school places in the area concerned.

So far, the Department for Education has received four sets of proposals from promoters which are under consideration, of which three are from existing independent schools – two RC and one interdenominational Christian. I understand that the Funding Agency for Schools is in active consultation with the proprietors of four further independent schools – two Sikh, one Muslim and one Seventh Day Adventist. Other independent schools have made informal contact with the Funding Agency for Schools and the Department for Education.

Although none of the interest shown so far from the private sector has come from ex-direct grant schools, you will be aware from a recent Parliamentary answer that six LEA schools which were former direct grant schools have joined the grant maintained sector.

Yours Ever,
John

George Walden Esq, CMG, MP

GEORGE WALDEN, C.M.G., M.P.

HOUSE OF COMMONS
LONDON SW1A 0AA

Rt. Hon. John Major, MP 14th March 1995
Prime Minister
10 Downing Street
London SW1

Dear Prime Minister,

Thank you for your reply of 20th February to my letter of 17th January about education. I note your wish for a "public sector of education that is second to none". I share that wish and have supported the Government's reforms. However, I believe it is illusory to speak of a "public sector second to none" in a country where for that most compulsive of human motivations – self-interest – the richest and most influential people have no personal incentive to work for higher aspirations in state schools.

We speak of "parent power", yet however many reforms we introduce there will be no serious shift away from the philosophy of low expectations that dominates many of our schools until the most powerful parents in the country have a stake in them. Noises of "concern" from outside the system are no substitute. Educationally we are therefore caught in a trap, in which talk of making the state sector as good as the private is an exercise in circular thinking and self-delusion. It is for this reason amongst others that I speak of a "blocked society".

The information in your letter confirms, by its very sparseness, that our educational blockage is set to continue. You provide no evidence of significant movement, either actual or potential, across the great divide. It is interesting to know that a Seventh Day Adventist school is considering entering the state sector, though I am sure you will agree that the kind of former direct grant school I referred to in my letter, of which there are 120 in the private sector, fall into a rather different category.

You were kind enough to describe my proposals as ''interesting and stimulating'', though I do not get the impression that they will be followed up in any way. I understand about money, though I can think of no greater priority than bridging our two-nation system of education. You will also have noted my suggestion that those who qualify for entry and are able to pay should contribute (as they do now by their fees) to any ex-private school that might move to the state sector. Expenditure on the Assisted Places Scheme might also be re-assessed. These measures would significantly lighten any new burden on the Treasury.

Tacit acceptance of the status quo, which is widespread on the left and the right, smacks to me of tacit defeatism. Being of a sunnily optimistic disposition I would like to believe that with will and imagination our education blockage could one day be broken. Whatever happens over Europe, without a first-class state education system, Britain will be a poor place to live, in every sense. What worked more or less in the past may not work in the future. A country of under-used talent and over-promoted mediocrity (an inevitable by-product of a two-nation system) will find the going increasingly harder in the world as it is going to be.

You were kind enough to read and comment on my first letter. Please do not trouble to reply again. I enclose a copy of a letter I am writing to Tony Blair on the same subject.

Yours ever,

GEORGE WALDEN, C.M.G., M.P.

HOUSE OF COMMONS
LONDON SW1A 0AA

Rt. Hon. Tony Blair, Esq., MP
Leader of HM Opposition
House of Commons
London SW1

16th March 1995

Dear Tony,

The purpose of this letter is not to score political points, but to seek to engage your interest in a matter on which in an ideal world there would be cross-party agreement: namely the structure of our education system.

By and large I support Government reforms and oppose much of what I understand to be Labour policy in the area. Naturally I am interested in signs of new thinking on your side of the House on such matters as grant-maintained schools, and, according to the press, on private schools too. I also note that you see education as the key issue in the country's future. So it is, which is why I am writing to your personally from the government back benches.

Despite our very different standpoints, I imagine you would sympathise with some of the views I express in the enclosed correspondence between myself and the Prime Minister, which I am publishing today. It is my impression that both you and John Major wish to improve state education. But whatever your different approaches, so long as the richest and most influential people in society opt out of the state sector, there will be severe limitations on what any political party can do to raise aspirations. This is not an ideological position, but a social fact. You will also note my reservations about the Assisted Places Scheme, which I have voiced in the House.

It is also my impression that you are moving away from what I would regard as a negative attitude towards private schools. Naturally I welcome this. Making life harder for these schools, many of which are excellent, would do nothing to help the state sector. And again it is a social fact that well-to-do parents would go to any lengths – as is their right – to continue to buy educational privilege for their children in one form or another.

I hope that this shift in Labour thinking, if such it is, will leave you open to more positive suggestions for bridging our two-nation system. It seems to me that there is a reluctance on both sides of the House, springing from antique conflicts and prejudices, to face up to the problems built up over the years by the public private stand-off. What cannot be discussed cannot be solved.

My proposal, in brief, is for the state to offer to "buy out" private day schools on a strictly voluntary basis. Initially, few would accept. In the short term probably only a handful of the former direct grant schools, of which there are 120 in the private sector, would return to the state system. Yet once the tendency was established more might follow: such schools would be pinnacles of excellence open to all, and provide stiff competition to private schools. There could be a cumulative effect. The long-term educational and social benefits of having more parents taking an interest in the state sector are obvious.

The gist of my proposal is:

a) Any private day school of sufficient academic standard could enter the state sector, in return for throwing its doors open to all the talents by examination. (Technically this is possible now, though for obvious reasons, mostly I suspect financial, little is happening).

b) The extra burden of financing such schools, whose per capita cost is often double that in the state sector, could be lightening by continuing to charge fees for those able to pay, and by re-assessing the Assisted Places Scheme.

c) Any school that took up the offer would have to be guaranteed continued independence: in effect something close to the old direct grant system.

I am wary of voucher schemes if only because, however attractive in theory, in the British case, middle-income parents would use them to go private. The result could be an even bigger gap between state and independent schools than before.

I would imagine it is the element of selection in my own proposal that would disturb some of your colleagues most. I am aware of all the arguments, but in the real world they are a recipe for the *status quo*. The stark fact is that no private school of any calibre is going to opt for the state system if it means going comprehensive. I genuinely fail to see why Labour should wish to allow a situation to continue in which many of the best schools in the country, formerly in the state sector, remain in effect the preserve of the well-to-do. Talent, diligence and intelligence, in whatever social stratum they lie, deserve to be rewarded by the best teaching, wherever it is to be found.

Contrary perhaps to appearances I have not one scintilla of naivety on the politics of the matter. Indeed it is because I am so aware of the traditional party stances that I am trying to introduce a little rationality into the discussion. I do not expect for one moment that you will receive my proposals with open arms – indeed in your position I might well send a studiously non-commital reply. All I seek is to do what little I can as a backbencher to encourage some new thinking and to promote a more constructive debate. If we are locked forever into old attitudes on education, God help our schools, and the country.

An obvious answer would be to say that money spent in enticing private schools into the state sector would be better spent on existing schools, to enable them to compete on a fairer basis. I am in favour of making education a spending priority. Yet I am sure you would agree that, in the end, what matter are educational structures and philosophies, rather than money alone. And to get them right you need the active involvement of all sections of society.

Finally may I say that I note and applaud your steadfast support for the Government's endeavours in Northern Ireland. It would be strange indeed if we were to succeed in overcoming tribalist thinking there, while perpetuating it in the country as a whole in the crucial field of education.

I am sending a copy of this letter for his information to Paddy Ashdown.

Yours ever.

Tony Blair replied to the preceding letter in a hand-written note to say that the ideas were interesting, and to suggest a meeting. This took place in his office on 6 April 1995. It was agreed that the discussion would remain private.

Paddy Ashdown replied saying he found the proposals interesting and had passed them on to his Education Spokesman, Don Foster.

Index

Index